Everything You

Always Wanted to Know About

JUDGMENT

But Were Too Busy Doing It to Notice

By Robert Perry and Allen Watson

Book #11 in a Series of Commentaries on
A Course in Miracles®

This is the eleventh book in a series, each of which deals with a particular theme from the modern spiritual teaching, *A Course in Miracles* ®. The books assume a familiarity with the Course, although they might be of benefit even if you have no acquaintance with the Course. If you would like a complete listing of these books and our other publications, a sample copy of our newsletter, or information about The Circle of Atonement, please contact us at the address below.

The Circle of Atonement
Teaching and Healing Center
P.O. Box 4238, West Sedona, AZ 86340
928-282-0790, Fax 928-282-0523
E-mail: info@circleofa.com
Website: http://nen.sedona.net/circleofa/

The ideas presented herein are the personal interpretation and understanding of the authors, and are not necessarily endorsed by the copyright holder of *A Course in Miracles*: Foundation for *A Course in Miracles*, 41397 Buecking Dr., Temecula, CA 92590. Portions from *A Course in Miracles*, © 1996, *Psychotherapy: Purpose, Process and Practice,* and *Song of Prayer*, © 1996, reprinted by permission of the copyright holder.

All references are given for the Second Edition of the Course, and are listed according to the numbering in the Course, rather than according to page numbers. Each reference begins with a letter, which denotes the particular volume or section of the Course and its extensions (T=Text, W=Workbook for Students, M=Manual for Teachers, C=Clarification of Terms, P=Psychotherapy, and S=Song of Prayer). After this letter comes a series of numbers, which differ from volume to volume:

T, P, or S-chapter.section.paragraph:sentence; e.g., T-24.VI.2:3-4.

W-part (I or II).lesson.paragraph:sentence; e.g., W-pI.182.4:1-2.

M or C-section.paragraph:sentence; e.g., C-2.5:2.

Copyright © 1995 by The Circle of Atonement

Second Printing 2002

All rights reserved

ISBN 1-886602-18-2

Published by The Circle of Atonement: Teaching and Healing Center
Printed in the United States of America

Cover art by James Francis Yax

Perry & Watson

CONTENTS

Introduction

Robert and Allen

Judgment is a central issue on the path laid out by *A Course in Miracles* and along the spiritual path in general. We all sense that judgment is in direct conflict with the journey's goal of absolute love. Yet still it feels impossible to get by in this world without it.

The keynote of the Course's attitude toward judgment is sounded in the following passage:

> The world's training is directed toward achieving a goal in direct opposition to that of our curriculum. The world trains for reliance on one's judgment as the criterion for maturity and strength. Our curriculum trains for the relinquishment of judgment as the necessary condition of salvation. (M-9.2:5-7)

The contrast between the way of the world and the way of the Course could not be more stark. In the world we are supposed to develop our capacity to make sound judgments and then rely on this faculty with increasing frequency and in ever weightier matters. This is "the criterion" for being judged a mature, capable adult. In the Course, we are trained to let the whole thing go. Letting go of judgment is "the necessary condition of salvation." Its reward is not the privilege of being judged a responsible adult; it is the joy of release from the bondage of the human condition.

This book is based on a weekend intensive presented by both of us in Sedona, in November, 1994. In it we try to briefly cover the major elements of the Course's treatment of judgment. We discuss many aspects of judgment: what it is; judgment in relation to others; why it must be let go; practicing non-judgment; some right uses of judgment that are encouraged by the Course; God's judgment; and the Last Judgment. As with many themes in the Course, judgment leads into nearly every aspect of the Course's thought system and practice.

In format, the intensive consisted of ten sessions given alternately by us. We have retained that format in this book; beneath each title of the ten chapters we indicate which of us wrote it. The book represents a condensed version of the intensive, perhaps only half of what was discussed in the live class. One consequence of this is that many passages that we read in full in the class are simply referred to with a footnoted reference in the book. Readers wishing to learn as much as possible from the study of this book are encouraged to look up these references in the Course. Some may wish to obtain the tapes of the intensive which are available from the Circle.

Chapter 1
What Is Judgment?

Robert

Among students of *A Course in Miracles* and spiritual students in general, "judgment" is a word that gets tossed around quite a lot. We know that we are supposed to not judge. We know that we should practice and cultivate non-judgment. Yet what is this creature we are supposed to give up? What is judgment?

As normally used, "judgment" seems to be a synonym for "condemnation." Yet I think the Course means something much broader by the word "judgment." It means a process of deciding what something is and how well it measures up. Judgment decides how good, worthy and desirable a thing is vs. how bad, worthless and undesirable it is. It decides if we should draw something close or push it away. In the end, it includes such diverse functions as condemning other people, interpreting their motives, interpreting our perceptual world and deciding on the most desirable course of action. Thus defined, judgment is a concept that is active in almost every single thought that ever crosses our minds. By examining the concept of judgment, then, we are grappling with a core issue in life.

In this chapter I would first like to describe the process of judgment, using eight steps. Second, I will discuss why the Course says that we can never know reality through judgment. Finally, I hope to show that pain is inherent in the act of judging. I will use the same eight steps to describe all three of these.

I. The Process of Judgment

The following outline attempts to describe why we judge, how we judge and what results from judgment. It describes this from the commonsense point of view of our everyday experience, rather than from the perspective of ultimate reality.

1. The First Law of Difference: We Are Separate from Things

Our experience is that everything is outside of us. Because things stand apart from us, their nature remains an enigma. Between us and all things outside exists a deep gulf of mystery. We do not know what they are, and so we need to figure them out.

2. The Second Law of Difference: Reality is Composed of a Variety of Different Things

It seems obvious that reality is a motley jumble of differences, in size, shape, weight, color, function and character. Since things are different, they will impact us differently. Some are positive and will impact us positively. Others are dangerous and will hurt us.

3. The Need to Judge

The need to judge is an inescapable result of the above two laws of difference. Since things can impact us differently, we must know which ones will affect us positively, so we can draw those things to us, and which ones will hurt us, so we can distance ourselves from them. Yet because we are separate from things, we don't know what they are. Thus arises the need to judge.

4. The Standard for Judgment

In order to judge, we need to measure things against a standard. A standard is a model or ideal, a concept of what something *should* be. The following insightful analysis comes from *Webster's Dictionary*:

> **Synonyms:** standard, criterion, gauge, yardstick, touchstone. Shared meaning element: a means of determining what a thing should be.

The Course discusses the concept of a standard using two terms: *goal* and *role*. First, we decide what a thing's goal is, what purpose or end it should serve. Then we decide *how* it should serve that end, what its specific role should be. We judge it by comparing it to this standard, by deciding how well it is playing its role and serving its goal.

According to the Course, we give all things the role of serving our "ego goals,"[1] our personal interests. In other words, the parent standard of all our standards is who we think we are and what we think we need. What everything *should* be is something that supports our identity, meets our needs and preserves our existence.

5. The Judgment

The judgment itself is a process consisting of several steps:

a. Accumulation of Evidence: We gather evidence about the thing we are judging.

b. Measurement Against the Standard: We measure the body of evidence against our chosen standard. We measure our evidence about what the thing *is* against our concept of what it *should be*.

c. Opinion: We arrive at a judgment, our opinion of what the thing actually is, what it means, how good, worthy, significant, desirable it is.

d. Sentencing: We arrive at a course of action that applies our judgment to the thing judged. This involves an entire additional judgment process.

e. Carrying Out the Sentence: We behaviorally act out the sentence.

The following two points expand on steps c, d and e.

6. Category I: The Punished/Rejected

In our judgment, certain things do not measure up to our standards. They are judged bad: guilty, worthless, undesirable, etc. Our response to them is two-fold:

a. Punishment: We treat them badly since this is what they deserve. They are evil, so they deserve evil.

b. Rejection: We reject them. We dispel them from our presence. We distance ourselves from them so that they cannot hurt us.

7. Category II: The Rewarded/Selected

Our judgment also decides that certain things are good: innocent, worthy, favorable, attractive, desirable, etc. Our response to these is also two-fold:

> *a. Reward:* We treat them favorably since this is what they deserve. They are good so they deserve good.
>
> *b. Selection:* We select them to be close to us, to be part of our lives. We draw them near to us so they can make us happy.

8. The Hierarchy of Preference

Through millions of judgments of what things are and of how one thing compares to another, we organize our existence. Our minds and our outer lives become organized according to a hierarchy, a personal caste system. This hierarchy of preference ranges from an inner circle of most desirable to an outer darkness of most contemptible.

It is not hard to see that this process pervades our entire lives. One could take anything in the human world and see how this process has shaped it. Perhaps the most obvious and direct example is the criminal justice system. There, it is assumed that because we are separate from people, who they really are and what they have actually done is a mystery to us (first law of difference). Yet it is imperative to find out, for people are different and therefore can impact us differently (second law of difference). Some can hurt us, some can become respectable neighbors. We find out who is who in court. There we weigh their actions against the standard of the law. As a result, a judgment is rendered. The guilty are punished and removed from society. The innocent are allowed to remain in society and are often compensated. Out of this process emerges a social hierarchy of the included and the excluded, the good citizens and the outcasts.

II. Reality Cannot Be Known Through Judgment

Judgment claims that it will let us know what things really are. That is how it gains our allegiance. Yet a closer examination shows that by its very nature judgment will never yield real knowledge. The following discussion covers the same eight points, but assumes not our commonsense experience of reality, but the Course's vision of true or ultimate reality.

1. We Are Not Separate and So We Need Not Judge

If we are truly outside something we can never *really* know what it is. Yet reality is not separate. Therefore, direct, experiential knowledge of the fundamental nature of everything is part of our being.

2. Reality Is Unity; There Are No Differences to Be Judged

Reality is a totality, a seamless oneness. There is no such thing as differences within it. Since judgment assumes differences, it blocks knowledge rather than revealing it.

3. Reality Can Only Be Accepted, Not Judged

Judgment never embraces whole-heartedly. It always picks and chooses. Yet to be known, reality can only be accepted, in its entirety and without reservation. "It is possible to look on reality without judgment and merely know that it is there."[2]

4. Our Standard Obscures Reality with Our Own Egocentric Ideas

Our standard of measurement is ruthlessly subjective. We measure everything against our apparent identity, its needs and its survival. This means that we judge everything based on how it impacts our ego, our false self. Can this result in knowing what anything really is in itself?

5. Judgment Is an Attempt to Be Special and to Play God

This is the key. Judgment is not really an attempt to know. Its true motivation is much darker, and that is why it fails to reveal knowledge. Judgment is our attempt to:

> *a. be above, be special:* The act of judging assumes that we are in a *position* to judge, subtly affirming that we are higher than what we judge. "…judgment…must come from someone 'better,' someone incapable of being like what he condemns, 'above' it, sinless by comparison."[3] Further, this desire to be special becomes a bias that guides our judgments. Our judgments therefore end up magically concluding that we are in fact better, higher, more special.

b. be the author of reality: In judgment we are not trying to find out what things are. We are trying to decree what they are. We are trying to play their creator. We are trying to usurp the function of God. "…if you wish to be the author of reality, you will insist on holding on to judgment."[4]

6. Category I: Rejection Leads to Blindness

"Judgment always involves rejection."[5] When we reject something and do not want it in our presence, we are saying we do not want to *know* it. It thus becomes distant and alien to our minds. Further, since reality is one, rejecting part of reality means rejecting all of reality. "And what he judges false he does not see. You who would judge reality cannot see it….The out of mind *is* out of sight."[6]

7. Category II: We Cannot Select Parts of Reality

Since reality is one without exception, the attempt to select and favor certain parts of it means losing sight of all of it—one of the fundamental flaws of special love.

8. The Only Hierarchies Are of Illusion

Since "There is no order in reality,"[7] by erecting our personal hierarchy we have lost sight of reality. We are left with an organized constellation of illusions, a kingdom that protects and pays tribute to its king, our personal ego.

III. The Agony of Judgment

The previous section described how judgment blinds us to reality. This of course causes great existential pain. Yet judgment also causes enormous pain on the mundane level of everyday life.

1. Separation Causes Pain

Judgment assumes separateness, and our sense of separateness from the things around *us* leads to the pain of loneliness, uncertainty and meaninglessness.

2. Seeing Differences Destroys Peace and Produces Fear

Differences are the potential for conflict. By seeing a world of differences we see a world wrought with conflict. This must destroy peace. A world of differences is also a world that can conflict with *us*. This must produce fear.

3. Our Need to Judge Affirms the Reality of Threat

We only need to judge when we perceive a reality that *cannot* be accepted without reservation, a reality filled with dangerous things which need to be identified and rebuffed. Judgment, being based on fear, reinforces fear.

4. Our Standard of Judgment Reinforces Ego and Ties Us to the Past

The ego—its needs and survival—is the standard by which we judge. All our judgment is thus an attempt to protect what we think we are. Yet what we think we are is the source of our pain. Further, "Judgment always rests on the past, for past experience is the basis on which you judge."[8] Judgment, therefore, repeats the past and preserves the ego as if frozen in time.

5. Trying to Be Special and to Play God Brings Guilt

By casting ourselves as the judge of the universe, we inherently sense that we are taking on a role that is too big for us, one that we cannot possibly assume in a responsible fashion. Assuming this role brings several forms of guilt:

> *a. Guilt over wrong judgments:* Since this role is too big for us, we live in fear of screwing it up.
>
> *b. Guilt over condemning judgments:* See point #6 below.
>
> *c. Guilt over trying to be better:* Judging is a subtle attempt to elevate ourselves above that which we judge. This causes guilt.
>
> *d. Guilt over trying to usurp God's function:* Every time we judge we sense that we are trying to steal God's role. We therefore feel guilty and fear that He will slaughter us.

6. Category I: Using Judgment Against Others Means Using It Against Ourselves

Having a category of people that we have judged worthy of punishment and rejection leads to guilt. In a cruel act of personal "justice," we condemn ourselves because we have condemned others. As a result, we need to get rid of all this self-condemnation, so we transfer this condemnation to others, condemning them even more. Yet this does not work, for we constantly fear that our condemnation will return to get us. "That is why those who project [condemnation] are vigilant for their own safety. They are afraid that their projections will return and hurt them."[9]

7. Category II: Even the Parts We Select We Do Not Appreciate

We cannot appreciate something when we tear it away from the totality. For its beauty and wholeness lie in its oneness with the whole. We also cannot appreciate it when we see it as existing for the sole purpose of pleasuring our little ego.

8. We End Up Living in Our Own Private World of Self-Made Illusions

"Thus does [the ego] assemble reality to its own capricious liking, offering for your seeking a picture whose likeness does not exist. For there is nothing in Heaven or earth that it resembles...."[10]

Summary

Judgment, therefore, is a patent failure at the two things it claims to deliver. It claims to reveal truth, but instead yields subjective, self-made illusions. It claims to protect us from pain, but it is the cause of our pain. After a lifetime of judging, we are left feeling lonely, empty and guilty.

---

1 W-pI.25.2:1
2 T-3.VI.9:6
3 T-24.I.4:2
4 T-3.VI.5:8
5 T-3.VI.2:4
6 T-13.VII.5:4-6
7 T-17.I.5:7
8 T-15.V.1:3
9 T-7.VIII.3:9-10
10 T-15.V.7:2-3

Chapter 2

Judgment Is Not Our Function

Allen

Judgment is not our function, but the function of the Holy Spirit. The following quotations state this basic premise clearly:

> I have said that judgment is the function of the Holy Spirit, and one He is perfectly equipped to fulfill.[1]

> To order is to judge, and to arrange by judgment. Therefore it is not your function, but the Holy Spirit's.[2]

Why Judgment Is Not Our Function

Let's look at a few reasons why judgment is not our function, but that of the Holy Spirit.

We Do Not Know Enough

We simply do not know enough to judge. Workbook Lesson 25 says, "I do not know what anything is for." Obviously we think we do know, and that is our problem. We know the purpose of things at a superficial level; for instance, we know what a telephone is for: talking to someone at a distance. "Yet purpose cannot be understood at these levels" (4:3). For instance, we don't understand why we want to reach someone by phone.

We may think we understand. You might be calling the Circle to order a book. But you see this purpose only from the point of view of your personal interest; what might be the purpose in the divine plan?

There is a deeper purpose in everything, a purpose of joining and salvation, that we do not understand. We cannot understand it as long as we think our conscious goals are the real ones. We have "to be willing to give up the goals [we] have established for everything" (5:1).

The entire foundation of our judgment is rotten because it rests on the idea that there are "things" outside us that differ from us. As long as we are coming from that false premise, our goals will be skewed and our judgments will be faulty, because there is nothing outside us; everything is part of us.

I find it very helpful to remember that I don't know what anything means and I don't know what it is for. A phone call may bring "bad news," but I can give up that evaluation and say, "I do not know what this phone call is for; I do not know what this situation is for, and therefore I cannot judge it."

The Course insists on our total ignorance. "The confusion between your real creation and what you have made of yourself is so profound that it has become literally impossible for you to know anything."[3] That's quite definite, isn't it? "Literally impossible." This isn't any figure of speech. Obviously, if you literally know nothing, judgment is impossible.

"Let us remember not our own ideas of what the world is for. We do not know."[4] If we don't know what anything is for, we can't judge it! We can't evaluate whether or not it is fulfilling its purpose because we don't know what its purpose is.

We aren't being asked to acquire all this knowledge we lack; the Course is asking us to become still and to remember how much we don't know.[5] The Text tells us that there is no statement that the world is more afraid to hear than this:

> I do not know the thing I am, and therefore do not know what I am doing, where I am, or how to look upon the world or on myself.[6]

It goes on to say that learning this is the birth of salvation. This is where learning starts: admitting how incapable of judging we are. Recognizing our ignorance is the birth of salvation because until we admit we don't know, we won't ask for help. As long as we think we know, we block true knowing.

> Little children recognize that they do not understand

> what they perceive, and so they ask what it means. Do not make the mistake of believing that you understand what you perceive, for its meaning is lost to you.... Yet while you think you know its meaning, you will see no need to ask it of Him.
>
> You do not know the meaning of anything you perceive. Not one thought you hold is wholly true. The recognition of this is your firm beginning.[7]

1. We Don't Have Wide Enough Knowledge

The third and fourth paragraphs of Chapter 10, in the Manual for Teachers, make a very strong point: "judgment in the usual sense is impossible."[8] It points out that to judge we would need to know many different things:

- All of the past
- Everything about the present
- All the future
- All effects of our judgment on everyone and everything involved in any way
- That there is no bias in your perception, so that your judgment would be wholly fair.

And the point is: *nobody* is able to do this. Therefore: *Nobody can judge fairly and accurately*. This isn't any abstract thing, it is obvious common sense.

We don't have the knowledge we would need to judge, and only in "grandiose fantasies"[9] would we think we do. But the Holy Spirit does have all that knowledge. He knows the past, present and future; He knows the outcome for everyone remotely concerned. His judgment is unbiased. Therefore, isn't it sensible to give judgment over into His hands?

2. We Don't Know Totality

Lesson 311 gives another reason why we cannot judge. We cannot see *totality*. That is, not only do we not know *enough*; we see what we do see as many separate parts instead of an integrated whole.

> Judgment was made to be a weapon used against the truth. It separates what it is being used against, and sets it off as if it were a thing apart. And then it makes of it what you would have it be. It judges what it cannot understand, because it cannot see totality and therefore judges falsely.[10]

Judgment sees reality as a jumble of different things that are separate from us, rather than a seamless Whole, with every part related. "It separates what it is being used against."

We can't know anything because we've confused ourselves with our egos. Our belief in our identity as separate beings, located in bodies, has become an unquestioned core belief behind our every thought. We evaluate everything in terms of ego goals.[11] Before we even begin to evaluate what anything means we have presupposed that, whatever it is and whatever it means, it is not us; it is *other*. From that premise it is *literally impossible* to know or understand anything *because it is not other*. It is part of us.

A very young baby in its crib goes through a process of learning that its foot or hand is part of itself. To begin with the baby does not know that. You can watch the baby, sometimes, treating the foot as if it were a foreign object.

We are all still infants in this sense because we don't recognize parts of ourselves when we see them; we think they are something else. Because we think they are something else, we are unable to form judgments that make any sense. Our judgments are not simply exaggerated or inaccurate, they are so wide of the mark they're ludicrous.

Because we are not seeing the totality, we cannot judge.

> There is only one way out of the world's thinking, just as there was only one way into it. Understand totally by understanding totality.[12]

Unless we understand totality our understanding is incomplete, and with incomplete understanding we are incapable of judging. Only the Holy Spirit understands totality; therefore, judgment is His function, not ours.

Our Judgment Is Prejudiced

Another reason judgment isn't our function is that our judgment is severely prejudiced.

The ego as a judge gives anything but an impartial judgment. When the ego calls on a witness, it has already made the witness an ally.[13]

> It is surely good advice to tell you not to judge what you do not understand. No one with a personal investment is a reliable witness, for truth to him has become what he wants it to be.[14]

When we identify with our ego, we prejudice our judgment. We see everything in terms of what it means to us, how it affects us, and in particular how it affects our ego identity. We don't trust somebody on the Federal Communications Commission if they own a TV station because they have a personal investment. We have a personal investment in our egos. Therefore, we are totally untrustworthy judges of anything.

Our Judgment Is an Illusion

Judgment is not our function because our senses deceive us. Read Lesson 151, the third and fourth paragraphs. They tell us that our judgment rests upon what our senses show us, and our senses give unreliable reports. "You place pathetic faith in what your eyes and ears report."[15]

This lesson teaches that we only have the illusion of judgment; we cannot judge at all. Our so-called judgment arises from the input of our unreliable senses. We know very well that our senses deceive us, and yet we continue to trust them and make judgments based on them. We are not seeing reality; we are seeing the ego's interpretations or judgments, projected onto the world. Therefore, the belief that we can judge is completely false.

Chapter 10 in the Manual is one of the key sections on judgment. In the second paragraph, it teaches us that in giving up judgment we are giving up an illusion. Better, we have an illusion of giving up something, because in giving up an illusion we give up nothing real; we just become more honest. We just recognize the impossibility of our judging anything, and stop trying to do it.

Reality Cannot Be Judged

Judgment is not our function because reality cannot be judged.

> In the end it does not matter whether your judgment is right or wrong. Either way you are placing your belief in the unreal. This cannot be avoided in any type of judgment, because it implies the belief that reality is yours to select *from*.[16]

We believe we have the right and power to decide what is real and what is not. We don't. Reality is not subject to judgment. Reality simply *is*. We can only accept what is so.

Attempting to judge reality makes it impossible for us to see reality. "Whenever judgment enters reality has slipped away."[17] Judgment is not a tool for finding out the truth; it is a tool for destroying it, or putting truth out of sight where the mind cannot recognize it.

What We Cannot Judge

Reality

I said above that we cannot judge reality; we can only accept it. To me it's a little like the weather. My judgment of the weather as good or bad is totally irrelevant to the weather. I cannot make rain go away because I don't like it. All that I can do is choose how to react to it. My judgment cannot change it. All I can do is to accept it as it is. I am not able to decide what is real and what isn't, and if I reject a part of reality, it changes nothing.

Motives of Others

We cannot judge the motives of others.

> ...analyzing the motives of others is hazardous to you....The analysis of ego-motivation is very complicated, very obscuring, and never without your own ego-involvement.[18]

We can't really understand anyone's ego motives because we see things through the distorting lens of our own ego. Analyzing another's ego is "hazardous to *you*," not to the other person. We end up reacting to illusions, and quite literally being out of touch with reality.

Our Thoughts

Later, we will discuss the fact that the Course does ask us to judge our thoughts. But this is not something we can do *by ourselves*. We need to bring our thoughts to the Holy Spirit and to ask His judgment on them, and then to accept His judgment.

> Bring, therefore, all your dark and secret thoughts to Him, and look upon them with Him. He holds the light, and you the darkness. They cannot coexist when both of You together look on them. His judgment must prevail, and He will give it to you as you join your perception to His.[19]

The early lessons in the Workbook give us exercises in refraining from judging our thoughts:

> The exercises consist, as before, in searching your mind for all the thoughts that are available to you, without selection or judgment. Try to avoid classification of any kind. In fact, if you find it helpful to do so, you might imagine that you are watching an oddly assorted procession going by, which has little if any personal meaning to you.[20]

Judging our thoughts by ourselves is an entrenched habit we need to break with this kind of practice. Once we learn to suspend our judgment, we can ask for His. Lesson 151 contains a wonderful description of how the Holy Spirit evaluates our thoughts. He removes the dream elements and gives the thoughts back "as clean ideas." "Give Him your thoughts, and He will give them back as miracles."[21]

Our Response to Any Situation

We cannot judge any situation, nor what to do in response. All such decisions are to be left to the Holy Spirit. (We'll say more about decision-making later.)

> The only way out of the error is to decide that you do not have to decide anything. Everything has been given you by God's decision.[22]

Today I will make no decisions by myself.

This means that you are choosing not to be the judge of what to do. But it must also mean you will not judge the situations where you will be called upon to make response.[23]

Judgment Belongs to the Holy Spirit

To sum up: Judgment is not our function because we do not have the equipment to judge with. Rather, judgment is the function of the Holy Spirit. He has the equipment with which to judge because His perception is perfect and without prejudice. He always judges in accord with reality; His judgment is always right; and His judgment does not produce illusions, but undoes them.

When the Holy Spirit judges, he always dismisses any case for condemnation:

> The ego speaks in judgment, and the Holy Spirit reverses its decision, much as a higher court has the power to reverse a lower court's decisions in this world.[24]

You need not fear the Higher Court will condemn you.…It will dismiss the case against you, however carefully you have built it up. The case may be fool-proof, but it is not God-proof.[25]

The Holy Spirit's only judgment is always the same: God's Son is guiltless. He sees everything as either love or a call for love.

---

1 T-8.VIII.4:7-9
2 T-14.X.5:8-9
3 T-3.V.3:2
4 T-31.I.12:2-3
5 T-31.II.6:4
6 T-31.V.17:7
7 T-11.VIII.2:1-2, 5; 3:1-3
8 M-10.3:1
9 M-10.3:7
10 W-pII.311.1:1-4
11 W-pI.25.2:1
12 T-7.VII.10:9-10
13 T-8.VIII.4:8-9
14 T-12.I.5:1-2
15 W-pI.151.3:5
16 T-3.VI.2:10-12
17 T-13.VII.5:5
18 T-12.I.1:6; 2:1
19 T-14.VII.6:8-11
20 W-pI.10.4:4-6
21 W-pI.151.14:1
22 T-7.X.6:8-9
23 T-30.I.2:2-4
24 T-5.VI.4:1
25 T-5.VI.10:1-6

Chapter 3
Differences as the Basis for Judgment

Robert

As we saw in Chapter 1, once we believe that reality consists of different things, we simply *must* judge. Imagine looking out and seeing your world teeming with differences, some things being safe and friendly, other things being vicious and deadly, some filled with significance, others utterly void of any meaning or relevance. In such a world, could you possibly refrain from judgment? Could you really resist the temptation to tell one thing apart from another? There is no way. That is why the Course acknowledges quite directly that

> ...difference of any kind imposes orders of reality, and a need to judge that cannot be escaped.[1]

Once there are differences, we must judge. We must. In this chapter we will look first at all the differences we believe in. And then we will examine how the Holy Spirit sees these same differences.

Our Perception Rests on Differences

Everything is different, has different names and identities

Although we just spoke of this situation hypothetically, it is not hypothetical at all. When we look out at our world we *do* see a place crowded from floor to ceiling with differences of every kind. "...the world's perception...rests on differences...thousands of contrasts in which each thing seen competes with every other in order to be recognized."[2]

Our most fundamental acknowledgment of these differences is our naming of things. "You have made up names for everything you see. Each one becomes a separate entity, identified by its own name. By this you carve it out of unity."[3] We attach great importance to these names. Getting someone's name wrong is considered an insult. We spend much of our lives, especially our childhoods, just learning all these different names. In fact, this is how the Course characterizes our educational system. "It is hard to teach the mind a thousand alien names, and thousands more. Yet you believe this is what learning means...."[4]

Different goals, roles and meanings

Once we assign something its own name, and so "carve it out of unity," we then assign it its own goal or purpose. We grant it its own special reason for existing. Not only do these purposes change from thing to thing, they vary from time to time.

As I mentioned in Chapter 1, on the basis of the purpose we assign something, we give it a role or function. This means we decide precisely *how* it should fulfill the purpose we have given it. These roles, like the purposes they serve, shift as frequently as do our moods. "The functions which the world esteems are so uncertain that they change ten times an hour at their most secure."[5]

Purpose and role then determine meaning. "Purpose is meaning."[6] In other words, what something means to us is determined by the purpose we assign to it and by how well we think it is living up to that purpose. By the time we are done assigning purpose, role and meaning, everything in the world means something different. We end up juggling literally thousands and thousands of meanings, which undulate and mutate both with the changing tides of the world and the changing whims of our minds.

> You add an element into the script you write for every minute in the day, and all that happens now means something else. You take away another element, and every meaning shifts accordingly.[7]

Different problems, answers and lessons

> The world seems to present you with a vast number of problems, each requiring a different answer....They

> seem to be on so many levels, in such varying forms and with such varied content, that they confront you with an impossible situation.[8]

Obviously, each distinct problem requires its own unique answer. And as we pass through one problem after another, we learn particular lessons from each one. In other words, we believe that each situation has a different lesson to teach us. Even if we don't believe in spiritual lessons that are "sent" to us, we still believe that different situations have different things to teach us.

Different responses to different people

Because everyone possesses a distinct character and is filled with their own special nuances of meaning, everyone merits a unique response from us. Just as different problems require different answers, so different people deserve different treatment. Some deserve reward, while others deserve rejection and punishment:

> The world solves problems in another way. It sees a resolution as a state in which it is decided who shall win and who shall lose....[9]

The Holy Spirit's Lack of Differences

We generally take the above differences for granted, and then we wonder how we can refrain from judging. The Holy Spirit has a completely different approach to the matter. In His perception, most of the differences that make judgment necessary simply do not exist.

He sees no differences in what is real

As was mentioned earlier, reality has no differences. "It has no separate parts and no degrees; no kinds nor levels, no divergencies and no distinctions. It is like itself, unchanged throughout."[10] On the practical level, this means that the Holy Spirit sees all people as the same (this refers to the real person or mind beyond the body and the personality). We not only have the same worth, the same abilities and the same needs, but we all share the same Self. Hence, although the Holy Spirit knows all the different names we use to refer to each other, He does not believe in them. "The Holy Spirit uses all of [the little names of the world], but He does not forget creation has one Name, one meaning, and a single Source which unifies all things within Itself."[11]

He sees no differences between illusions

When we look at the physical world, we see a vast assortment of objects of diverse sizes and shape, with distinctive meanings and purposes and different grades of significance. When the Holy Spirit looks at our world He sees something else entirely. He sees a whole lot of nothing. Just different sizes and shapes of nothing. Since it all is nothing, it is all the same. And this is what we will see when our mind is healed.

> The body's eyes will continue to see differences. But the mind that has let itself be healed will no longer acknowledge them....Just as reality is wholly real, apart from size and shape and time and place—for differences cannot exist within it—so too are illusions without distinctions.[12]

He sees only one difference—between reality and illusion

If there are no differences within reality and no differences between illusions, the conclusion is inescapable: Only one single difference exists—the difference between reality and illusion. This difference *does* require judgment: "sorting out...the false from the true...is a process of separation in the constructive sense...."[13] Yet it is the Holy Spirit, not ourselves, Who makes this judgment. "His function is to distinguish only between the false and the true, replacing the false with the true."[14]

Every person, object, event and situation has one purpose and one meaning

Even though there is an unbridgeable gulf between what is real and what is illusory, there is one sense in which they are one: They have the same purpose. Our minds have a completely different reality status than our bodies. Our minds are an eternally real part of God, while our bodies are utterly illusory. *Yet both share the purpose of salvation.* The purpose of our minds is to find salvation; the purpose of our bodies is to be used as instruments in attaining this goal. Thus the real mind and the illusory body are united in sharing a single purpose. This is true for all the real minds and all the illusory bodies, objects, events and situations in this world. They all share the purpose of salvation.

> The Holy Spirit looks upon the world as with on purpose, changelessly established....A common purpose is the only means whereby perception can be stabilized, and one interpretation given to the world and all experiences here....Escape from judgment simply lies in this; all things have but one purpose, which you share with all the world.[15]

Since all things have one purpose, they all have one meaning. "You do not have to judge, for you have learned one meaning has been given everything, and you are glad to see it everywhere."[16]

> Seeing with Him will show you that all meaning, including yours, comes not from double vision, but from the gentle fusing of everything into *one* meaning, one emotion and one purpose.[17]

There is only one problem, one answer and one lesson

Behind the myriad problems of our lives there is only one problem. "The problem of separation...is really the only problem."[18] No matter what their form, how big or small, whether they seem to be spiritual problems, mental problems or physical problems, all our problems are just different forms of the one belief that we are separate from our Creator.

If there is one problem there is only one answer. "One problem, one solution."[19] Further, no matter how varied situations may seem to be, they all contain only a single lesson. "The Holy Spirit teaches one lesson, and applies it to all individuals in all situations."[20]

> Each lesson has a central thought, the same in all of them. The form alone is changed, with different circumstances and events; with different characters and different themes, apparent but not real. They are the same in fundamental content. It is this: "*Forgive, and you will see this differently.*"[21]

Everyone deserves the same response—the gift of everything

Because everyone is the same in all true respects, everyone deserves the exact same response: the maximal power of God's total love. "...being always maximal, it offers everything to every call from anyone."[22]

> Each miracle is an example of what justice can accomplish when it is offered to everyone alike....Because it does not make the same unlike, it sees no differences [between people] where none exists. And thus it is the same for everyone, because it sees no differences in them. Its offering is universal, and it teaches but one message: *What is God's belongs to everyone, and is his due.*[23]

Summary

Because we believe we live in a world of tremendous differences, it appears that an unrelenting series of judgments is required of us. We *have* to engage in these judgments, or so it seems. We must decide what something is, what it is for, what it means and what it should be. We must evaluate problems, figure out their exact nature and devise appropriate responses. We must decide what lesson we should learn from each problematic situation, so that next time we will be better equipped. And, perhaps most important of all, we must decide who is deserving of our love, who is not, and when.

But what if none of these differences existed? We would not have to judge! There would be nothing *to* judge. Imagine the freedom and relief that would result if you did not have to shoulder the constant responsibility of judgment. This, according to the Holy Spirit, is exactly the situation that is facing us. Everything is the same. Every person has the same worth, the same needs and the same Self. Therefore everyone deserves the same absolute love, all the time and in every situation. Imagine being able to assume that someone deserves total love, before you even met him, before you found out the slightest thing about him. Imagine being freed of the burden of having to decide between people. The Course says that this is why we invented perception in the first place. "You made perception that you might choose among your brothers...."[24] What, then, would happen to perception if we stopped choosing among our brothers?

True, there is *one* difference, that between reality and illusion. And this *does* need to be judged. But the Holy Spirit will do that for us. If we will only open our minds to His quiet but certain promptings, He will unerringly discern for us what is real and what is mere appearance.

Moving on to the realm of appearances, of illusion, again, differences do not exist. All things we see with our eyes—all forms and events—are the same. There is no need to judge between them, to figure out which is good and which is bad. They are all nothing.

There is also no need to decide what anything should be or what purpose it should serve. Everything has the same purpose. "Escape from judgment simply lies in this; all things have but one purpose, which you share with all the world."[25] There is no need to decide what anything means: "You do not have to judge, for you have learned one meaning has been given everything...."[26] We do not have to figure out what each individual problem is; they are all the same problem. We do not have to creatively devise answers, for all problems have the same identical answer, the same lesson to teach us: *"Forgive, and you will see this differently."*

Because differences are unreal, we can drop the burden of judgment right here and right now. We can stop judging and be free.

1 T-24.I.3:6
2 M-8.1:1-2
3 W-pI.184.1:2-4
4 W-pI.184.5:2-3
5 W-pI.186.10:4
6 W-pI.25.1:1
7 T-30.VII.1:7-8
8 W-pI.79.4:2; 5:2
9 T-25.IX.4:4-5
10 W-pI.127.1:4-5
11 W-pI.184.11:3
12 M-8.6:1-2,7
13 T-2.VIII.4:1-2
14 T-8.IX.5:4
15 T-30.VII.1:4; 4:1; 5:1
16 T-30.VII.4:3
17 T-14.VII.7:5
18 W-pI.79.1:4
19 W-pI.80.1:5
20 T-7.III.1:1
21 W-pI.193.3-7
22 T-14.X.6:13
23 T-25.IX.10:4, 7-10
24 T-21.III.6:5
25 T-30.VII.5:1
26 T-30.VII.4:3

Chapter 4
Judging Others

Allen

The Foundation of Judgment Is the Belief in Sin

To understand why we judge others in the sense of condemning them, we need to review Course metaphysics, because judgment stems from our belief in sin and separation.

In the beginning there was oneness and God; this oneness is called Heaven. God extended Himself to create the Son of God, but all was still one; there is nowhere that the Father leaves off and the Son begins. Since there is no separation in Heaven, there can be no differences; and where there are no differences, there can be no judgment. Something happened, therefore, or seemed to happen, to make judgment possible.

Into Heaven, where all is one, there crept a tiny, mad idea: the idea that separation from the Father is possible.[1] The idea, however, was not the problem. The problem came when the Son believed that the idea could really be accomplished and have real effects. The Son forgot to laugh at the idea; instead, he took it seriously. The power of his mind made it seem real, although in truth nothing actually happened.

When the illusion of effects, of seeming separation, became "real" in the mind, the concept of "sin" had just been invented. If sin existed, the Course says, to sin would be "to violate reality, and to succeed."[2] That is exactly what our mind believed had happened.

> [Sin] assumes the Son of God is guilty, and has thus succeeded in losing his innocence and making himself

> what God created not.…Sin is the grand illusion underlying all the ego's grandiosity.[3]

Sin is the ego's foundation. The Course calls it "a major tenet in the ego's insane religion,"[4] "wholly sacrosant to its thought system, and quite unapproachable except with reverence and awe."[5] Sin is the idea of separation made real; without it the ego does not exist, and so the ego will protect the concept of sin in every way it can.

Once the idea of sin had been accepted, guilt and fear were sure to follow, and with them, judgment. Guilt is simply the emotional reaction you feel when you believe that you have sinned and made yourself a bad person who deserves to be punished. If sin is real, guilt is justified. And if you are guilty, you will fear punishment; you will fear the consequences of your action.

> Punishment is always the great preserver of sin, treating it with respect and honoring its enormity. What must be punished, must be true.[6]

The ego lives by guilt.[7] No guilt, no ego. Therefore the ego wants to hold on to guilt and to increase it. However, our mind cannot tolerate the massive guilt that belief in separation induces. Therefore the ego gives us a way that seems to reduce guilt, although its true purpose is to keep guilt in our minds. The ego teaches us to deny guilt in ourselves and to project it outside. By seeing others as guilty, we think we will be less guilty. "You gave him not his holiness, but tried to see your sins in him to save yourself."[8] That is the origin of *judgment* in the sense of condemnation.

Read the Introduction to Chapter 13 of the Text. It says, "If you did not feel guilty you could not attack, for condemnation [judgment] is the root of attack." Feeling guilty leads us to judge others; judging others is the root of attacking them because they deserve to be punished. So judging others rests firmly on our belief in the reality of sin.

Once you believe that *you* have denied God and separated yourself from Him, your mind wants "to deny itself [i.e. to deny oneness or separate] and escape the penalty of denial."[9] How will it do that? "Believing that by punishing another, it will escape punishment."[10] That's judgment: We believe we can reject our own nature, and yet escape the penalty by deflecting the penalty onto someone else. And that is *why* we judge one another. Everything can be traced back to that metaphysical moment, that first mistake:

> Yet in each unforgiving act or thought, **in every judgment** and in all belief in sin, **is that one instant still called back**, as if it could be made again in time.[11] (My emphasis.)

We really cannot judge, and any apparent effects of judgment are unreal. If judgment is an illusion, then why do we deal with it?

> To condemn is thus impossible in truth. What seems to be its influence and its effects have not occurred at all. Yet must we deal with them a while as if they had. Illusion makes illusion. Except one. Forgiveness is illusion that is answer to the rest.[12]

So although judgment is really impossible, and the effects of judgment never really happened, "yet must we deal with them a while as if they had." We deal with it through forgiveness, which is a kind of counter-illusion.

Judging Others Serves to Keep Us Separate

We are judging in order to keep ourselves separate. To justify our separateness we must judge our brothers as unworthy and undesirable. In vivid imagery, the Course paints a picture of us wielding a sword of judgment in order to maintain the illusion of separation.[13]

It is the illusion of ourselves as separate that holds us apart from our brothers. To maintain that illusion of ego we *must* judge. Judgment is the weapon we use, the sword with which we "fight to keep the space that holds your brother off unoccupied by love."[14]

> Idle wishes and grievances are partners or co-makers in picturing the world you see. The wishes of the ego gave rise to it, and the ego's need for grievances, which are necessary to maintain it, peoples it with figures that seem to attack you and call for "righteous" judgment. These figures become the middlemen the ego employs to traffic in grievances.[15]

The ego's "need for grievances" is what makes the world and people in it seem to be worthy of judgment. Grievances, or judgments, are "necessary to maintain" the illusion of separation.

We judge because we want to. Judgment is nothing but an ego device designed to keep the separation going. It is designed to hold guilt in place in our minds by deflecting it onto others, and in the process causing us to see them as different from ourselves, and separate from us.

We choose attack, or judgment, in order to preserve and maintain our belief in separation. And we want the belief in separation in order to feel safe about our attack. It's a vicious circle.

> And this belief you want [separateness]. Yet wherein lies its value, except in the desire to attack in safety?...You would not choose attack on its [the universe's] reality if it were not essential to attack to see it separated from its maker.[16]

We really think there are "other minds" out there that we can judge without affecting ourselves. "The dreary, hopeless thought that you can make attacks on others and escape yourself has nailed you to the cross."[17]

> It seems to you that other people are apart from you, and able to behave in ways which have no bearing on your thoughts, nor yours on theirs. Therefore, your attitudes have no effect on them, and their appeals for help are not in any way related to your own. You further think that they can sin without affecting your perception of yourself, while you can judge their sin, and yet remain apart from condemnation and at peace.[18]

It really does seem that way to most of us, doesn't it? The Course is saying, by implication, that the opposite is true. There are no other people apart from us. They can't behave in ways that have no bearing on our thoughts; our thoughts have a direct effect on them. Their calls for help are very closely related to our own calls for help, and when we try to distinguish between them we are deluding ourselves. We want to see our own problems as calls for help while we continue to judge theirs as damnable sins, but we cannot do that.[19]

We Judge to Establish Specialness

Separateness is closely related to *specialness*. We don't want only to be separate; we want to be special, not just set apart but set above others. Judgment is a perfectly marvellous way to feel special. The more I can condemn others, the more special I feel.

> Only the special could have enemies, for they are different and not the same. And difference of any kind imposes orders of reality, and a need to judge that cannot be escaped.
>
> What God created cannot be attacked, for there is nothing in the universe unlike itself. But what is different calls for judgment, and this must come from someone "better," someone incapable of being like what he condemns, "above" it, sinless by comparison with it.[20]

The desire to be special is what makes enemies; being better requires someone to diminish. By judging we can feel "better" or "above" what we condemn. I strengthen my specialness by condemning you.

In every judgment "is the voice of specialness heard clearly, judging against the Christ…." [21] Every time you judge you are hearing the voice of specialness. Every little thought that makes you feel superior to anyone is a thought of specialness.

Because we are not separate, judging to maintain specialness does not work. The judgment we lay on others always applies to ourselves. We are wielding the sword of judgment. We think it is against others, but really we are holding the sword over our own heads.[22]

Judging Others Is Really Self-Judgment

All judgment is self-judgment, and this is so in two senses.

First, your judgment on another person is always the projection of your judgment on yourself. You are judging others *because* you have judged yourself and feel guilt. If you were not trying to get rid of your own guilt, you would not attack or judge at all.

> The world you see is but a judgment on yourself. It is not there at all. Yet judgment lays a sentence on it, justifies it

> and makes it real. Such is the world you see; a judgment on yourself, and made by you.[23]

(See also Text, p. 415; T-21.IN. 2:1–5 and Workbook Lesson 22.)

Second, when you attack another you are actually attacking yourself. What you are attacking is really a projected image of your own guilt. Furthermore, you are attacking the Christ, and you are the Christ. "All attack is Self attack."[24]

Look at Text, p. 170; T-10.II.4, 5. (Please note that paragraph five was omitted from the 1st edition.) These paragraphs tell us that we are actively choosing not to remember our own true identification, and even not to remember God. It is an active thing, not passive. We are judging against our true self in every judgment. This is not easy to see because we don't want to see it. Seeing our self-attack in every attack, however, is crucial, because if we don't see it, the attack will appear to be out of our control.

Judging another is attacking yourself because you are seeing yourself as an attacker instead of an extension of Love; you are "teaching yourself that you are not what you are." So "You always attack yourself first."[25] You are attacking your identification with Christ, Who cannot attack.

Judging Is Making the Error Real

> That is why analyzing the motives of others is hazardous to you. If you decide that someone is really trying to attack you or desert you or enslave you [i.e. you have judged them], you will respond as if he had actually done so, having made his error real to you. To interpret error is to give it power, and having done this you will overlook truth.[26]

When you judge another person you are making their error real. The other person mistakenly thinks they are an ego in a body, and they are acting to preserve their ego self. They want love but think they want something else, and they are attacking you, thinking that is the way to get what they want. They cannot truly attack you, but they can imagine they are attacking you, and imagination can be very convincing. When you react as if what they did is really attack, or desertion, or betrayal, you are confirming their mistake. You are believing that their mind is truly evil, and no longer the perfect creation of God. That is what judgment does; it makes error "real."

> To perceive errors in anyone, and to react to them as if they were real, is to make them real to you.... Accept his errors as real, and you have attacked yourself.[27]

The Course concept of "making the error real" means to see someone else's errors and react to them as if they were real. Judgment does not mean simply seeing and identifying what someone is doing. If you tell a lie and I say, "You are lying," that is not a judgment; that is a fact. If I react to you as if *you are a liar*, however, that is judgment. If I cut you out of my heart because of what you did, that is making the error real.

You make the error real when you hold a grievance. You make the error real when you react to the error in any way. The Course says we do not join with someone else's illusions, but we do join with *them*. You make the error real when you separate yourself, not just from their behavior, but from who they are. When you judge, you are refusing to join with the person, and you *are* joining with their illusion about themselves; you are rejecting the truth and making the error real in its place.

Others Are Our Mirrors

How we see one another is simply a mirror for how we see ourselves.

> As you see him you will see yourself. As you treat him you will treat yourself. As you think of him you will think of yourself. Never forget this, for in him you will find yourself or lose yourself.[28]

The way you see another person in judgment is a picture of what the ego wants to make of *you*. When you find yourself judging, ask yourself, "Is this how I want to see *myself*?" That is the real meaning of the question in Workbook Lesson 134, "Would I condemn myself for doing this?"[29] It means, "Do I want to lay this judgment on myself? Do I want to see myself the way I am seeing my brother?"

Because when you judge, you *are* laying the judgment on yourself. Later in the lesson it is stated more clearly:

> Would I accuse myself of doing this? I will not lay this chain upon myself.[30]

When you are judging another you are laying chains on yourself; he is your mirror, and the way you treat him is a reflection of how your own ego is attacking *you*.

> But forget not this; the role you give to him is given you, and you will walk the way you pointed out to him because it is your judgment on yourself.[31]

---

1 T-27.VIII.6:2
2 T-19.II.2:2
3 T-19.II.2:4,6
4 T-19.II.4:1
5 T-19.II.5:2
6 T-19.III.2:4-5
7 T-13.I.2:5
8 T-22.III.8:6
9 T-13.Int.1:5
10 T-13.Int.1:4
11 T-26.V.5:5
12 W-pI.198.2:5-10
13 T-31.VII.9:1-3
14 T-31.VII.9:2
15 W-pI.73.2:1-3
16 T-22.VI.12, read whole paragraph
17 W-pI.196.5:1
18 W-pI.126.2:2-4
19 T-27.II.13:4-6
20 T-24.I.3:5-6; 4:1-2
21 T-24.VI.13:2
22 W-pI.192.9:4
23 T-20.III.5:2-5
24 T-10.II.5:1
25 T-10.II.4:5
26 T-12.I.1:6-8
27 T-9.III.6:7; 7:2
28 T-8.III.4:2-5
29 W-pI.134.15:3
30 W-pI.134.17:4-5
31 T-25.V.6:6

Chapter 5
Judging the Motives of Others

Robert

I doubt that we realize just how much of our lives is spent trying to figure out the motives of others. Though not formally taught, this is one of the most highly valued skills on the planet. Long before we reach adulthood we have become quite sophisticated in sniffing out what other people are really up to. As they stand before us, we take in every subtle cue available: words, intonation, pauses, facial expression, direction of gaze, gestures, body posture. As they speak we develop theories about what is really motivating them. We test our theories by asking them crucial test questions or giving them telling opportunites, to see how they will respond. And this is only the beginning. Once they are gone we plug all the data from that conversation into the master computer, which remembers literally everything they have ever done to us and everything we have ever heard about them from others. If, after processing the new conversation in light of the master data bank, we still do not understand what exactly is motivating them, we will meet to discuss the issue with others, perhaps for hours. Finally, after all this investigative work, we will most likely have a theory that we are quite sure of. And whether we are right or not, we will treat that person *as if* we know what is motivating them.

It takes all of this effort because we are trying to solve very difficult questions. To begin with, there must be thousands of possible answers, since any particular motive is a complex mixture of more basic motivations. Further, motivations are generally well hidden beneath surface appearances carefully devised to give the wrong impression. Even the person himself is not aware of all that is motivating him. Finally, we all know that we have personal biases, making the whole enterprise even more difficult and complicated.

Yet, it is worth it nonetheless, or so we tell ourselves. For we are trying to solve questions of such great consequence: Does she really love me? Will he really commit? What will I have to give her to get what I want from her? Is he really considering firing me? What inner motivation is really driving her to adopt this opinion or make that decision?

We *must* figure out the motivation, because, if we don't, we will not know what their action means and so we will not know how to respond. And if we do not know how to respond, how will we protect ourselves from attack? How will we even know it is coming? Additionally, how will we know how to identify the elusive key to our happiness, should it happen to cross our path? And how will we know when good things are being done to us, so that we can thank and encourage them and thus keep them coming? In short, if we do not interpret people's motives, how can we build a life in which we are surrounded by niceness and pleasure and protected from meanness and danger?

Though we are attentive to both positive and negative (as we consider positive and negative), we seem to be much more concerned with the negative, with looking out for "evil." In trying to interpret motivation, therefore, our foremost question seems to be: *How much evil intention was involved*? We imagine this evil existing everywhere, skulking behind every smile and apparently generous act. Thus preoccupied, we tend to overlook loving motivations, for we do not trust them. We suspect that they are no more than a cover for something much darker. "Nor does he trust the 'good' in anyone, believing that the 'bad' must lurk behind."[1] As a result, we often see the gifts of others as "loans at best; at worst, deceptions which would cheat you of defenses."[2]

In fact, basic to the Course's theory of perception is the idea that 1) we see what we look for and 2) what we look for is *sin*. There is a powerful discussion of this in the section entitled "The Obstacles to Peace."[3] There it talks about how "the hungry dogs of fear" (15:6) are sent out to search for sin and guilt in the world, and then carry it back to feed their master, fear. This is actually a metaphor for how our own belief in fear guides our attention, directing our eyes to search for and focus on sin and guilt in the world, which, once found, is feasted on by our mind in order to feed our fear.

Looking at our process of interpreting the motives of others, it is clear that we mentally act as our own personal penal system. Our mind goes out on patrol to look for criminals, apprehend suspects and bring them before the judge and jury, where their actions and motives are judged. Finally, of course, we carry out the sentence, which sometimes means rewarding people for good behavior, but most often means punishing and imprisoning them until they have paid their debt to us. The penal systems that we erect on a societal level, then, are simply the outpicturing of what we are all busy doing in our individual minds.

The Judgment of the Holy Spirit

The Course says flat out that we should not engage in "analyzing the motives of others."[4] "The analysis of ego-motivation is very complicated, very obscuring, and never without your own ego-involvement."[5] How can we possibly refrain from interpreting the motives of others? How could we survive in the world? The rest of the chapter will briefly attempt to address this. For, according to the Course, there is an alternative. The Holy Spirit's way of looking at the world does not involve such analysis. He does not see thousands of different motivations. And He does not see sin, guilt or evil at all. In His sight, these things do not exist. Just as in general He sees only the two categories of reality and illusion, so He sees only two categories of human motivation.

> There is but one interpretation of motivation that makes any sense. And because it is the Holy Spirit's judgment it requires no effort at all on your part. Every loving thought is true. Everything else is an appeal for healing and help, regardless of the form it takes.[6]

The only judgment involved is the Holy Spirit's one division into two categories; "one of love, and the other the call for love."[7]

This is a familiar idea to most students of the Course, and is one that has an immediate ring of intuitive truth. On some level we all realize that people are either extending love or are calling for love. Yet no matter how readily we sense the truth in this idea, it is quite another matter to consistently apply it. But just imagine if we did. No one could ever do or say anything to us, no matter how apparently cruel, that would anger or rile us, or would draw any response from us except love. There are several important points to make about this way of seeing.

The two categories of human motivation are reflections of the Holy Spirit's two basic categories

As we saw in Chapter 3, the Holy Spirit sees things in terms of only two categories: reality and illusion. All human motivation—loving and unloving—falls under the category of illusion. For motivation is thought, and all thoughts outside of Heaven are ultimately unreal. Yet within the illusory realm of human motivation some thoughts lead toward reality and some toward illusion. Thus the Holy Spirit's division of all motivation into two categories reflects His overall distinction between reality and illusion.

There are no distinctions within each category

This is one of the most radical elements in the Holy Spirit's judgment. He sees all expressions of love as the same. And He sees all calls for love as the same. Just as there are no differences between illusions, so different calls for love are not really different.

> The miracle offers exactly the same response to every call for help. It does not judge the call. It merely recognizes what it is, and answers accordingly. It does not consider which call is louder or greater or more important.[8]

In other words, heart-rending grief is no bigger a call for love than is minor irritation. The murderous rage that a "killer" feels is no less valid a call for love than is the pain that his "victim" feels. The gift that is given just to make the giver look holy is no less a call for love than is a burglar's act of stealing. The Holy Spirit sees them all as exactly the same. If there were any differences in calls for love, *then some would be harder to answer than others*. As a result there would be an order of difficulty in miracles.

Both categories evoke only a single response—love

The division between love and calls for love does serve a purpose. For on a *form* level we are meant to respond differently to the two different kinds of motivation. To the expression of love we respond with gratitude. To the call for love we respond with healing, with the miracle. This difference is indicated in the following passage:

> For those already willing to change their minds he [the teacher of God] has no function except to rejoice with them, for they have become teachers of God with him. He has, however, a more specific function for those who do not understand what healing is....To them God's teachers come...to remind them of the remedy God has already given them.[9]

Yet even though we respond differently to expressions of love and calls for love, the basic content of our response is the same. We respond with love. And love contains *both* gratitude *and* healing. The gratitude we offer to those who give us love contains power to heal their minds. And the healing we offer to those who call for love contains gratitude for "bringing love into [our] awareness."

Only appreciation is an appropriate response to your brother. Gratitude is due him for both his loving thoughts and his appeals for help, for both are capable of bringing love into your awareness if you perceive them truly....There is but one response to reality, for reality evokes no conflict at all.[10]

A beautiful simplicity, then, results from these two categories, if truly embodied. In essence, we have only one response to everything. We don't have to judge who deserves our love and who does not. We don't have to decide who to embrace and who to recoil from, who to favor and who to punish. We have only one reply to every living mind: an unreserved, whole-hearted "yes."

This involves only one judgment, which the Holy Spirit makes for us

At this point any "sane" person would be wondering how we can ever achieve such a lofty perception of the motivation of others. The Course's answer to this is: we can't. We must step aside and allow the Holy Spirit to judge through us.

> You cannot safely make this division [between expressions of love and calls for love], for you are much too confused either to recognize love, or to believe that everything else is nothing but a call for love. You are too bound to form, and not to content.[11]

This remark cuts to the heart of the matter. We cannot reliably identify love, for love to us is generally some behavior that protects our ego and grants its wishes. And we certainly do not believe that everything besides love is simply a call for love—since calls for love on a behavioral level are *attacks*. In essence, if our ego feels attacked, we call it sin. If our ego is pleased, we call it love.

The Holy Spirit has to tell the difference for us. I believe this starts with consciously suspending our interpretations and asking Him to see someone's behavior for us. It means saying, "Let me see this through Your eyes." Only through frequent practice in this over a long period do we reach the stage where His seeing through us becomes an unconscious habit. When this occurs, says the Course, even our thoughts will be ordered by the Holy Spirit, since He will be thinking through us. We will not have some thoughts that seem "more important, larger or better, wiser, or more productive and valuable than others."[12] We will have only two classes of thoughts about the world: "That was love" and "That was a call for love."

We are meant to look for and focus on the expressions of love

Earlier we discussed our propensity to look for sin and guilt in the world, to watch out for danger and seek for evidence of evil. We said that this search specifically guides our attention and even directs our physical eyes as we survey our world. The Holy Spirit's focus could not be more diametrically opposite. He is just as selective in His perception and searches just as actively to find what He is looking for. But He is looking for love. He is searching for acts of giving, charity and forgiveness. "He will select the elements...which represent the truth, and disregard those aspects which reflect but idle dreams."[13] The following moving passage speaks directly about what to focus on in the actions of others:

> Dream of your brother's kindnesses instead of dwelling in your dreams on his mistakes. Select his thoughtfulness to dream about instead of counting up the hurts he gave. Forgive him his illusions, and give thanks to him for all

> the helpfulness he gave. And do not brush aside his many gifts because he is not perfect in your dreams.[14]

What then does the Holy Spirit do with thoughts that are mixtures of the two categories, that express love *and* call for love at the same time? This is an important question, for precious few thoughts in this world are just pure and untainted love. In light of the above we can safely say that the Holy Spirit selects the love and disregards the rest. Thoughts that are "partly in accord with [the Kingdom] He accepts and purifies."[15]

> I have saved all your kindnesses and every loving thought you ever had. I have purified them of the errors that hid their light, and kept them for you in their own perfect radiance.[16]

Imagine seeing people strictly in the light of their most generous and egoless acts. Imagine seeing their past as nothing but a radiant string of kind and loving thoughts. This is how the Holy Spirit sees others and this is how He sees us.

Summary

In the Holy Spirit's judgment, the world takes on a profound simplicity. As we saw in Chapter 3, "difference of any kind imposes orders of reality, and a need to judge that cannot be escaped."[17] If the thousands of presumed differences in human motivation do not exist, we don't have to judge them all. We can merely assume, without examining any evidence, that someone is either giving love or calling for love. True, this does leave us one difference to decide. There is one judgment to make. But the Holy Spirit will make that one for us. Again, we don't have to judge.

The Course is offering a vision in which we are totally spared one of the oldest, most cherished and most draining of all human pastimes: interpreting the motives of others. The Course is promising that there is a way to go through life and never have to engage in that process. Instead, we can live in a world of simplicity and innocence, in which we never have to interpret someone's motives, in which we never have to judge, analyze or suspect the people around us, in which our one response is love.

1 T-31.VII.1:7
2 W-pI.197.1:5
3 For the discussion itself, see T-19.IV(A)11-15
4 T-12.I.1:6
5 T-12.I.2:1
6 T-12.I.3:1-4
7 T-14.X.7:1
8 T-14.X.6:3-6
9 M-5.III.1:4-5; 2:1,7
10 T-12.I.6:1-2,5
11 T-14.X.7:2-3
12 T-14.X.4:3
13 W-pI.151.11:1
14 T-27.VII.15:3-6
15 T-6.V(C).1:4
16 T-5.IV.8:3-4
17 T-24.I.3:6

Chapter 6

The Meaning of Seeing Without Judgment

Allen

Denying Guilt in All Forms

Judgment comes from belief in sin and guilt. If we did not have guilt in our minds, there would be no guilt to project and no reason to judge. Therefore, to see without judgment we must deny guilt in all its forms. The mind must become free from guilt, because as long as guilt is in the mind, it will be projected, and we will judge the projections we see.

> As long as you believe that guilt is justified in any way, in anyone, whatever he may do, you will not look within, where you would always find Atonement.[1]

In this chapter, therefore, we are going to be looking at giving up judgment as undoing our projection of guilt. To undo our projection of guilt there must be two steps:

- First, we must realize that the guilt we think we see in others is always our own guilt, projected out. All guilt is my own guilt.
- Second, the guilt must be undone and let go by bringing it to the Holy Spirit and with His vision seeing through its illusion. "Blame must be undone, not seen elsewhere."[2]

Seeing From a New Frame of Reference

The Holy Spirit is the key to true judgment. When we suspend all the ego's judgments, we accept His judgment in their place. Seeing without judgment is not difficult when we use *His* seeing instead of our own:

> There is but one interpretation [i.e. judgment]... that makes any sense. And because it is the Holy Spirit's judgment it requires no effort at all on your part.[3]

The ego always projects. From the ego's frame of reference you *cannot avoid* judgment; you need a completely new frame of reference in order to see without judgment. The Holy Spirit, God's Answer to our insane request for specialness, provides that new frame of reference:

> For His answer is the reference point beyond illusions, from which you can look back on them and see them as insane. But seek this place and you will find it, for Love is in you and will lead you there.[4]

The Holy Spirit is the "reference point beyond illusions." Forgiveness, or letting go of judgment, does not mean simply that we stop being critical and judgmental. It is an extreme, all-encompassing change of reference point from the ego's world view to the Holy Spirit's world view. It is the most extreme form of what has been called a "paradigm shift." A "paradigm" is a template or pattern. The ego's reference point is a basic pattern of thought that obliges everything perceived to fit into its form.

Imagine an invisible plastic grid with only certain open slots. If you drop marbles at random onto the grid they fall into a certain visible pattern, defined by the grid. A mental paradigm is like that. Whatever comes at our mind, the paradigm compels things to fall into particular slots. What we need is a new mental grid; a new frame of reference entirely. We don't simply need to move some marbles from one slot to another; we need to replace the grid.

The shift in frame of reference from ego to Holy Spirit is the most extreme paradigm shift that is imaginable. Letting go of judgment in a given situation is really not a gradual process, it is a radical shift into an entirely different state of mind. Diane Berke, in her book *Love Always Answers*, uses the example of "figure-ground" drawings:

> ...line drawings in which two different images can be seen in the same drawing. Probably the best known of these is a drawing that can be seen either as two faces in profile looking at each other or as a wine goblet.

She points out that we usually see only one image at first, and may not even believe the second image is there. "Until we see it ourselves, it isn't real to us, it doesn't exist for us in our experience." She continues:

> What is necessary in order to see the second image in a figure-ground drawing is to let go of our definition, our idea of what we are looking at. We need to let go of the mind-set that has interpreted what our eyes are physically seeing in a particular way. Letting go, we essentially return our perception to a state of innocence, of not knowing what we are looking at. In that freshness and openness, we suddenly see the second image, as if it had been revealed to our sight. Once we've seen it, it is hard to imagine ever having not been able to see it that way.
> (page 54)

The "figure-ground" shift is a radical change in the frame of reference. What was foreground becomes the background, and what was background becomes foreground. Forgiveness is like that. You cannot see what the Holy Spirit sees while you are holding on to your own perception. You need, as Diane says, to let go of your definition, your idea of what you are looking at, and see it with no preconceptions. When you are willing to do that, the vision of the Holy Spirit "snaps" into place.

> The holy instant reflects His knowing by bringing all perception out of the past, thus removing the frame of reference you have built by which to judge your brothers. Once this is gone, the Holy Spirit substitutes His frame of reference for it. His frame of reference is simply God.[5]

Lesson 151 speaks of letting the Holy Spirit judge for us. I'll quote just one paragraph, but I encourage you to read paragraphs 8 through 11:

> He will select the elements in them [your thoughts] which represent the truth, and disregard those aspects which reflect but idle dreams. And He will reinterpret all

> you see, and all occurrences, each circumstance, and every happening that seems to touch on you in any way from His one frame of reference, wholly unified and sure. And you will see the love beyond the hate, the constancy in change, the pure in sin, and only Heaven's blessing on the world.[6]

Seeing What Is There Without Evaluating

We aren't asked to judge as the Holy Spirit judges. He does the judging, and that is why it takes no effort on our part. Our only part *is not interfering* with His judgment by imposing our own. The Holy Spirit asks only that we look at things *without evaluating them*, that we "be innocent of judgment."[7]

If we withdraw the "ancient learning" of our judgment we leave a blank slate on which the Holy Spirit can write His interpretation. We let ourselves become "unaware of any thoughts of evil or of good that ever crossed [our minds] of anyone." We deliberately *forget* "all things we ever learned." We let those things "be loosened from our minds and swept away." Our willingness to have the interference removed is all that is asked; the Holy Spirit does the rest. He sweeps away all the images of judgment from our minds and replaces them with His vision.

To see without judgment means that you see neither bad nor good. You see everything as neutral, as without meaning, and you allow the Holy Spirit to show you the meaning. You look at everything and say:

> *I do not know what anything, including this, means. And so I do not know how to respond to it. And I will not use my own past learning as the light to guide me now.*[8]

When you say that, you open the way to the judgment of the Holy Spirit:

> By this refusal to attempt to teach yourself what you do not know, the Guide Whom God has given you will speak to you. He will take His rightful place in your awareness the instant you abandon it, and offer it to Him.[9]

So when something comes up, give it to the Holy Spirit for His judgment:

> Confronted with such seeming uncertainty of meaning, judge it not. Remember the holy Presence of the One given to you to be the Source of judgment. Give it to Him to judge for you, and say:
>
> *Take this from me and look upon it, judging it for me. Let me not see it as a sign of sin and death, nor use it for destruction. Teach me how* **not** *to make of it an obstacle to peace, but let You use it for me, to facilitate its coming.*[10]

The Holy Spirit Judges Behavior and Motives of Others

As Robert pointed out in the last chapter, when we judge the behavior and motives of others, we inevitably condemn them; our frame of reference demands it. When the Holy Spirit interprets them, He sorts out the loving from the unloving and overlooks the unloving as meaningless.

Although we are told to overlook our brothers' illusions and see their attacks as calls for love, we aren't supposed to be naive. Most people around us are nasty sometimes because, like us, they haven't learned their lessons yet. We need to be aware that everyone has an ego, and egos can be vicious. We do not become doormats, but neither do we counterattack. Someone who lacks learning does not need punishment, he needs teaching, and what will our attack teach him? Nothing but more attack. Those who make mistakes need to be helped, not punished. Our response of love and forgiveness, rather than attack and punishment, will teach and help them by showing them another way.

When the Holy Spirit judges through us, we lift people up out of their insanity by seeing their sanity for them. We see their reality as far beyond their appearance, and we reflect that reality to them:

> Charity is a way of perceiving the perfection of another even if you cannot perceive it in yourself....Charity is a way of looking at another as if he had already gone far beyond his actual accomplishments in time. Since his

> own thinking is faulty he cannot see the Atonement for himself, or he would have no need of charity. The charity that is accorded him is both an acknowledgment that he needs help, and a recognition that he will accept it.[11]

Seeing Without Judgment Is Forgiveness

Not judging is forgiveness, or overlooking mistakes. Learning forgiveness is learning to relinquish judgment.

Part II of the Workbook begins with "What is Forgiveness?," which presents a clear picture of unforgiveness and forgiveness.[12] It says:

> An unforgiving thought is one which makes a judgment that it will not raise to doubt, although it is not true. The mind is closed, and will not be released. The [unforgiving] thought protects projection, tightening its chains.... (paragraph 2)

Unforgiving thoughts make judgments and will not question them. That is really all we are asked to do: Raise our judgments to doubt. Remind ourselves that perhaps there is another way of looking at this. We need to open our closed minds.

> Forgiveness, on the other hand, is still, and quietly does nothing. It offends no aspects of reality [it does not try to impose a meaning on reality that it does not have; it does not select bits and reject other bits], nor seeks to twist it to appearances it likes. It merely looks, and waits, and judges not. (paragraph 4)

That is what forgiveness does: looks, and waits, and judges not. It suspends judgment. It sees what is there without evaluating it. It waits for the Holy Spirit to write His meaning on the blank slate.

Letting Judgment Go Is Essential to Salvation

Letting judgment go is the major learning goal of the Course's curriculum, and not just a side issue.[13]

The Manual for Teachers says that the one lesson we learn with increasing thoroughness is to listen to the Holy Spirit and follow His guidance.

> This becomes easier and easier, as the teacher of God learns to give up his own judgment. The giving up of judgment, the obvious prerequisite for hearing God's Voice....[14]

So learning to listen to the Holy Spirit becomes easier as we give up our own judgment. We have to suspend our own evaluations before we can hear the Holy Spirit. It is a "prerequisite." And giving up judgment "is usually a fairly slow process, not because it is difficult, but because it is apt to be perceived as personally insulting."[15]

I used to think that giving up judgment was a beginner's lesson. But it isn't something we can learn to do overnight. Although the shift in frame of reference is instantaneous, learning to consistently give up judgment is a *process*, and it is *fairly slow* because we have enormous resistance to doing so. In fact, when we actually achieve giving up judgment completely, we will be done with the journey!

> The world's training is directed toward achieving a goal in direct opposition to that of our curriculum. The world trains for reliance on one's judgment as the criterion for maturity and strength. Our curriculum trains for the relinquishment of judgment as the necessary condition of salvation.[16]

Although we learn it slowly, giving up judgment is "the necessary condition for salvation." It has to happen. If we give up judgment we will experience salvation; if we don't give it up, we won't experience salvation.

The full relinquishment of judgment comes at the very end of our development as a teacher of God.

> The centrality of open-mindedness, perhaps the last of the attributes the teacher of God acquires, is easily understood when its relation to forgiveness is recognized. Open-mindedness comes with lack of judgment.[17]

We become open-minded when we "let go all things that would prevent forgiveness,"[18] that is, let go of our judgments. Once we have let go of judgment, our mind is open to receive the judgment of the

Holy Spirit, and we see Christ in our brothers and ourselves. Thus letting go of judgment, being open-minded, forgiveness, and seeing the face of Christ are all related. Achieving one perfectly means achieving all of them; this is "the final goal of the curriculum."[19] Letting go of judgment, then, is something we are going to be working on until we've graduated.

In the section on "Development of Trust"[20] the Course says we may be in the next-to-last stage of this process for a long time. Why? *Because moving past it means giving up all our judgment*!

> And now he must attain a state that may remain impossible to reach for a long, long time. He must learn to lay all judgment aside, and ask only what he really wants in every circumstance.[21]

Giving up judgment, then, is central to the Course's teaching, and doing it completely is to learn the whole Course and graduate from school into the real world. It should be a primary focus of our training program. We should not despair if it seems to take a long time; it may take a "long, *long*" time. That is expected. But our dedication to let go of judgment should not be diminished by the thought of how long it will take. We can do this. We all will do this. The outcome is certain, and as we see how much pain judgment brings us we will become willing to give it up entirely.

---

1 T-13.X.6:1; see also 6:2-7:3
2 T-11.IV.5:3
3 T-12.I.3:1-2
4 T-13.III.12:9-10
5 T-15.V. 9:3–5
6 W-pI.151.11:1-3
7 T-31.I. 12:1-13:5
8 T-14.XI.6:7-9
9 T-14.XI.6:10-11
10 T-19.IV(C).11:5-10
11 T-2.V.9:4; 10:1-3
12 Page 401. This is the first of the one-page question-answer pages in the second half of the Workbook, and not a daily lesson. The "correct" reference is W-pII.1, which is singularly unhelpful. I therefore use only page numbers in referring to these question-answer sections.
13 M-9.2:7; M-10.3:1
14 M-9.2:3-4
15 M-9:2:4
16 M-9.2:5-7
17 M-4.X.1:1-2; read through 2:2
18 M-4.X.2:2
19 M-4.X.2:9
20 M-4.I
21 M-4.I(A).7:7-8

Chapter 7
Using Judgment to Arrange Our Lives

Robert

There is a certain kind of judgment that absolutely cannot be escaped in this world. Decisions must be made about the specifics of our lives. Choices about what to do and what to include in our lives are necessary. Even the Course acknowledges this: "There are decisions to make here, and they must be made whether they be illusions or not."[1] Doing anything requires a judgment which evaluates our options and decides that a certain action is more preferable than other actions. Even sitting still and doing nothing requires a judgment that you would rather sit still than get up.

The Course does not deny that this kind of judgment must occur. It simply says that *we should not do it*, making two points about this. First, the Holy Spirit is perfectly equipped to make every judgment for us. Second, judgment is a disaster in our hands. Let us look first at what the Course says about our use of judgment. The section entitled, "The Forgiving Dream"[2] offers a chilling vision of our process of arranging our earthly lives. (Unless otherwise specified, all quotations in the following section are from "The Forgiving Dream," numbered according to paragraph and sentence.)

Erecting Our Hierarchy of Preference

In Chapter 1 we spoke of using judgment to eresct our personal hierarchy of preference. None of us questions the need to do this. One of the most basic facts of conventional existence is that we must decide what belongs in our lives and what does not. We must weigh alternatives carefully and come up with good judgments about what is dangerous and what is beneficial. Over time we must build a life that surrounds us with what we prefer and distances us from what we deplore.

This seems like an innocent enough process. Yet there are far deeper forces involved in this process than any of us would initially suspect. These forces go down to the foundations of our personal identity. For it is judgment that sparked the entire separation. "A dream of judgment came into the mind that God created perfect as Himself. And in that dream was Heaven changed to hell..." (2:1–2).

Judging what belongs in our lives entails inherent attack, for some things, some people, *must* be rejected. In fact, *most* must be. To build a life we must push certain things away from us, judging them unfit, unwanted and dangerous. The Course characterizes this selection process as a childish game:

> The dream of judgment is a children's game, in which the child becomes the father, powerful, but with the little wisdom of a child. What hurts him is destroyed; what helps him, blessed. Except he judges this as does a child, who does not know what hurts and what will heal.
>
> (6:4–6)

The unavoidable result of judging against something is guilt, self-condemnation. In other words, we turn judgment against ourselves and decide we are worthy of being punished.

Then comes a crucial move. We project our self-judgment onto the things we have judged against, leading us to imagine that they too condemn us. We unconsciously cast them in the role of our punishers, of dispensing to us our rightful penalty.

For example, let's say that John really wanted to be part of your life, but you rejected him, deciding that he just wasn't worthy. Somewhere inside, you will feel guilt for judging against him, and you will feel that you deserve punishment. You will then project this belief onto him, imagining that he too believes you deserve punishment. This projection onto him is far more important than what he actually believes. "Everyone you attack keeps it and cherishes it by holding it against you. Whether he does this or does it not will make no difference; you will think he does."[3] Even if John in fact does hold it against you, your projection will add into your image of him the crucial affirmation that he is *right*, that you *do* have it coming to you. And that John should be its emissary.

So what do we do? What do we all do? Do we just lay down and accept what we believe we have coming? Or do we perhaps abandon the whole system of judgment? Of course not! We recruit body guards. We hire a whole collection of preferred people, situations, objects and events whose job is to protect us from the punishment we feel we deserve.

The Course calls these "idols." Specifically, they are things that we think will make us happy; things, like the idols of old, which we hope will answer our prayers and supply our needs. An idol is a special person that we believe will make us feel special. Or a new car that will give us the feeling of power. Or a high-level job that will confer upon us new status. All of the things we select to be in our lives are idols.

Basic to the purpose of our idols is protecting us from the pain of this world, pain that we are unconsciously convinced is just punishment for all our sins. Their purpose is to "hold the judgment off from resting on [your]self" (2:7); "to save you from what you believe you have accomplished, and have done to make you sinful and put out the light within you" (4:2). Idols "are...your salvation from the judgment laid in terror and in guilt upon yourself" (2:9); "idols...are interposed between your judgment and the penalty it brings" (3:7).

How do they protect us? Well, certainly they protect us physically. But more importantly they protect us emotionally. They make the statement that all those things out there that want to punish us are *wrong* about us. Isn't that what we hire them for? They are the defenders of our honor. They are supposed to stick up for us, to proclaim to us and all the world that those rotten people who mistreated us were gravely mistaken. They do this by actively defending us, by "loving" us and by simply staying in our lives. They are our "haven in the storm of guilt."[4] And the more special they are and the more special they think we are, the more effectively they shelter us from this storm.

There is another way in which idols protect us. They carry our thoughts of judgment for us. Initially, we rejected certain things and tried to dispel them from our lives. Now it is the job of the *idols* to dispel these things from our lives. Now they are the judge and jailer of all those things that we judged. They are judging *for* us. Why? "...because he fears his thoughts and gives them to the toys [the idols] instead" (5:5). Our judgments have frightened us, so rather than let them go, we let the idols carry them for us. We let our husband judge our parents for us. We let our wife hate our boss for us. They are our hired hit-men. We give our idols our thoughts of judgment just as we gave the things we rejected our thoughts of *self*-judgment.

But the problem with the whole system lies here. If we have given the idols our thoughts of judgment, how could we not also give them our thoughts of *self*-judgment?

To put it another way, we have *identified* with the idols. They carry out *our* function (of dispelling the bad things) and furnish us with *our* identity (of being someone wrongly accused). In our minds, then, our idols represent our "'true' identity" (2:9). Yet we have betrayed ourselves. By judging, we have violated our own best interests and made ourselves guilty. If we have been betrayed *by* ourselves, and we see the idols *as* ourselves, what will we expect the idols to do *to* us?

> Whenever you feel fear in any form...be sure you made an idol, and believe it will betray you. For beneath your hope that it will save you lie the guilt and pain of self-betrayal and uncertainty, so deep and bitter that the dream cannot conceal completely all your sense of doom. Your self-betrayal must result in fear [of being betrayed].... (9:1–3)

In other words, our friends, lovers, children, co-workers, homes, houseplants, cars, toasters, jobs, furniture, etc., have been subtly hired by us to betray us. On a surface level, we have hired them to protect us from our punishers. But on a deeper level, we have employed them to do to us what we have done to ourselves, what our punishers would do to us, what we fear God will do to us. We have asked them to punish and condemn us; only it is worse when we get it from them. We expect it from our enemies. But a bullet in the chest from an enemy is nothing compared to a knife in the back from a friend. When an enemy does it, that's just life. But when a friend does it, it's betrayal.

Yet this is how the dream works. Superficially, it is made of our desire to be happy, safe and free from fear. Yet on a deeper level, it is made of our *attraction* to fear. We *want* to be afraid, for fear keeps alive the ego, which "is quite literally a fearful thought."[5] Thus even the things we hire to protect us from fear also symbolize our attraction to fear. This is perhaps the scariest thing of all, when we realize that all that we fear is planted in the very things we employ to protect us, the very people we surround ourselves with to be safe, the very chosen few we invite into our inner sanctum.

The Course is quite clear that people do not *really* betray us. In its pages, Jesus refutes one of history's most famous stories of betrayal:

> Nor could they have described my reactions to Judas as they did, if they had really understood me. I could not have said, "Betrayest thou the Son of Man with a kiss?" unless I believed in betrayal. The whole message of the crucifixion was simply that I did not.[6]

The real story behind the apparent betrayals in our lives is our *attraction* to betrayal. It is this unconscious attraction that gathers to ourselves people who will play this part for us. It is this attraction that then covertly solicits them to perform certain behaviors. Finally, it is this same attraction that interprets those behaviors—which are really just calls for love—as betrayal.

Between our conscious desire for safety and our unconscious attraction to fear is stretched the entire human condition. We constantly try to bring only good things to ourselves. Yet danger is always lurking just outside the walls, marching and singing in the torchlight, from time to time breaching the walls and flooding in. Even more frightening than its frontal attacks are its attempts to infiltrate our own ranks; sending in spies and confederates, and worming its way into the souls of our dearest comrades. With one hand we push it away. But our lives are mute testimony to the fact that with another, stronger hand we are constantly pulling it toward us.

The diagram on page 57 illustrates this idea and the main ideas from the foregoing discussion.

Being Guided by the Holy Spirit

Building our lives using our own judgment yields frightening results: the terrifying condition we all live in. It is not a real alternative to do nothing and make no choices, for (besides the fact that no one is going to do that) even this requires a decision. The only true alternative is to let the Holy Spirit judge for us. His judgment can take care of all the things that our judgment attempts to. It will build a life for us, but it will be a very different life than one we build for ourselves. His guiding motivation will not be the protection and maintenance of our ego, but the very opposite: the relinquishment and transcendence of it.

He will judge for us. The Course promises that, and we all have experienced that on different occasions. Of course, the point most everyone brings up when they hear this is: How can I hear His Voice? There are a great many things that could be said in answer to that. But perhaps in the context of our current subject of judgment, the most important point to make is the one Allen made in the last chapter: *We hear His judgment to the extent that we let go of our own.* At one point the Course calls "the giving up of judgment" "the obvious prerequisite for hearing God's Voice."[7] Elsewhere it says, "As judgment shuts the mind against God's Teacher, so open-mindedness invites Him to come in."[8]

When I want to be guided by the Holy Spirit rather than by my own arbitrary preferences, I have found it helpful to mentally go through the following list of "I don't knows" in my mind, so helpful in fact that I found it useful to memorize it.

I don't know what the problem is

> Whenever any difficulty seems to rise, tell yourself quickly: "*Let me recognize this problem so it can be solved.*" Then try to suspend all judgment about what the problem is.[9]

I don't know what the question is

> Any specific question involves a large number of assumptions which inevitably limit the answer. A specific question is actually a decision about the kind of answer that is acceptable....Answers are not up to you. Any limit you place on them interferes with hearing. God's Voice is silent and speaks in silence. That means that you do not phrase the question and you do not restrict the answer [personal guidance given to Helen by Jesus].[10]

I don't know what this situation is for

...With your eyes resting on each subject you so select, say, for example:

> *I do not know what this chair is for.*
> *I do not know what this pencil is for.*
> *I do not know what this hand is for.*[11]

I don't know what the roles are here

What is your brother for? You do not know, because your function is obscure to you. Do not ascribe a role to him that you imagine would bring happiness to you.[12]

I don't know what this means

When your peace is threatened or disturbed in any way, say to yourself:

> *I do not know what anything, including this, means. And so I do not know how to respond to it. And I will not use my own past learning as the light to guide me now.*[13]

I don't know what my needs are

Everything the ego tells you that you need will hurt you....Therefore ask not of yourself what you need, for you do not know, and your advice to yourself will hurt you. For what you think you need will merely serve to tighten up your world against the light, and render you unwilling to question the value that this world can really hold for you.[14]

Your function here is only to decide against deciding what you want, in recognition that you do not know.[15]

I don't know what I am

There is no statement that the world is more afraid to hear than this:

> *I do not know the thing I am, and therefore do not know what I am doing, where I am, or how to look upon the world or on myself.*

Yet in this learning is salvation born. And What you are will tell you of Itself.[16]

My Name, O Father, still is known to You. I have forgotten It, and do not know where I am going, who I am, or what it is I do. Remind me, Father, now, for I am weary of the world I see.[17]

---

1 S-1.I.2:4
2 T-29.IX
3 T-14.III.5:5-6
4 T-16.IV.3:1
5 T-5.V.3:7
6 T-6.I.15:4-6
7 M-9.2:4
8 M-4.X.1:3
9 W-pI.79.10:2-3
10 See Absence from Felicity, p. 445, 450.
11 W-pI.25.6:3-6
12 T-29.IV.6:1-3
13 T-14.XI.6:6-9
14 T-13.VII.11
15 T-14.IV.5:2
16 T-31.V.17:6-9
17 W-pII.224.2:1-3

THE HIERARCHY OF PREFERENCE

A LIFE CONSTRUCTED BY PERSONAL JUDGMENT

1. **OUTER SECTORS**—unwanted people, things, events, situations, places, etc.—things we have judged against. Symbolize the punishment we think we deserve for judging. Symbolize our self-judgment.

2. **SECTOR SPILLS**—intrusions of outer sector material (unwanted people, thing, events, etc.) into our lives, despite our best efforts.

3. **IDOLS**—residents of the core sector. Wanted people, things, events, etc. **Nice face**: symbolizes their assigned role of protecting us from the outer sectors. **Evil face**: symbolizes unconsciously assigned role of betraying us and, like the outer sectors, punishing us for our judgments.

Chapter 8

The Right Use of Judgment

Allen

Judging the Ego

There is a sense in which the Course not only says we can judge, it says we *should* judge. It calls this "the right use of judgment" in Chapter 4 of the Text. Jesus is saying that our goal should be nothing less than shining away the ego. And then he says this:

> Watch your mind carefully for any beliefs that hinder its accomplishment, and step away from them. Judge how well you have done this by your own feelings, for this is the **one right use of judgment**. Judgment, like any other defense, can be used to attack or protect; to hurt or to heal. **The ego *should* be brought to judgment** and found wanting there. Without your own allegiance, protection and love, the ego cannot exist. Let it be judged truly and you must withdraw allegiance, protection and love from it.[1] (Bold is my emphasis.)

The right use of judgment is to bring the ego to judgment. The content of the right use of judgment is judging against the ego, but it takes several different forms, as we shall see.

How can this passage tell us to judge, when elsewhere the Course says that we cannot judge? Notice it says that this is *the one* right use of judgment. This is an exception to the rule, and the exception is typical of many similar exceptions in the Course.

The Holy Spirit uses the things the ego made in order to teach us the opposite of the lessons the ego wants us to learn. He says we can't decide anything alone, and yet He tells us to decide not to decide anything.[2] We think our mind has been changed by sin; He tells us that the mind is changeless, and that the only change of mind necessary is to change our mind about our mind, and so learn that it is changeless. Likewise, regarding judgment, He is saying that there is only one judgment we need to make: to judge against judgment. The ego is a thought of judgment, and in judging against the ego we are judging against judgment.

> Sane judgment would inevitably judge against the ego, and must be obliterated by the ego in the interest of self-preservation.[3]

Judging Our Emotions as Indicators

As we read in the first passage quoted above, we are to gauge how well we have watched our mind by our own feelings; this is "the right use of judgment." Our feelings are like a barometer of our state of mind. Unpleasant feelings are simply the result of thoughts; they call us back to vigilance concerning our thoughts. A disturbance in our peace is a sign that, whether we are aware of it or not, some judgment has been accepted by the mind:

> Certain it is that all distress does not appear to be but unforgiveness. Yet that is the content underneath the form.[4]

Evaluating our emotions and feelings is a specific form of judging the ego. In particular the Course calls on us to judge whether or not we like the *results* of listening to the ego. We are told that if we forget, judge by ourselves, and find we aren't willing to let it go, we can get unstuck by reminding ourselves, "At least I can decide I do not like what I feel now."[5] That paves the way for the next step, which is: "*And so I hope I have been wrong*."[6] Hoping we have been wrong leads us to realize that we *want* another way to look at the situation.

For instance, perhaps a friend really lets me down in some big way, and I feel really resentful about it. I "try" to forget about it but it keeps nagging at me. Every time the memory comes up, every time I see my friend, the resentment surfaces.

When I'm stuck in a grievance loop like that, the way out is to judge my feelings honestly. *Do I like the way I am feeling*? The initial sweetness of anger quickly turns sour and bitter. Unforgiveness is a rancid, ugly feeling. Think about the physical symptoms that accompany anger: a flushed face, a throbbing in the head, a tightness in the chest, a churning in the belly, a pounding of the heart. Do you *like* feeling like that? Of course not. Recognizing that you do not like the feelings generated by the ego can open the door to a change of mind.

Judging What We Want

We are always making judgments about what we want. The ego always tries to get what it wants, and the ego wants guilt and fear. With the help of the Holy Spirit we can judge our thoughts to see if they are leading to guilt and fear. If they are, we can ask for help in changing them, recognizing that it is the ego, and not ourselves, that wants these things.

> Look calmly at the logical conclusion of the ego's thought system and judge whether its offering is really what you want, for this *is* what it offers you.[7]

What the ego is offering us is explained in the previous paragraph: a perception of ourselves as "a sick god, self-created, self-sufficient, very vicious and very vulnerable."[8] That is the "logical conclusion of the ego's thought system," and the Course is asking us to judge whether or not that is what we really want for ourselves. The answer is "No," of course.

This is simply another aspect of judging the ego and finding it wanting; in this case, judging its goals and realizing they are exactly what we do not want. We can judge how we treat others, and realize that the condemnation we appear to want for them is what our ego wants for us. "Teach no one that he is what you would not want to be."[9] We can look at what we are teaching our brother, and judge if that is what we want for ourselves.

Judging Against the Illusions of the Ego

> To know reality must involve the willingness to judge unreality for what it is. To overlook nothingness is merely to judge it correctly, and because of your ability to evaluate it truly, to let it go.[10]

Another aspect of the one right use of judgment is judging unreality for what it is: unreal. This is the way to deal with any illusion of the ego, for instance, thoughts of anxiety in the mind.

Judging Against Illusory Thoughts

Once I woke up at about 3:30 in the morning, worrying about how I would pay some bills. The more I fought against the thoughts the more they kept churning in my mind. The presence of this deep anxiety in me disturbed me, as a student of the Course. I thought I was beyond such things.

Then, the Holy Spirit reminded me: "These thoughts do not mean anything." It was as if a sudden weight were lifted off my back. I thought that having such anxious thoughts showed that I was a poor learner or maybe even a hypocrite. But, looking at them with the Holy Spirit, I saw that they were meaningless. I clearly remember saying out loud, "Oh!" And then almost immediately I fell back to sleep.

We have learned certain ways of thinking until they have become habit. Now the Course is asking us to judge what we have learned.

> Your past learning must have taught you the wrong things, simply because it has not made you happy. On this basis alone its value should be questioned. If learning aims at change, and that is always its purpose, are you satisfied with the changes your learning has brought you?[11]

That is a kind of judgment: Has what I have learned made me happy? Is thinking along these lines making me happy? If not, a change is indicated: "If the outcome of yours [your curriculum] has made you unhappy, and if you want a different one, a change in the curriculum is obviously necessary."[12]

Judging Against the World We Made

Judging the illusions of the ego extends to the entire world we have made. "Everyone will ultimately look upon his own creations and choose to preserve only what is good."[13] There is a sense in which we must judge our world and choose to retain only the good, only that which was created with God, and to reject all that we made without Him. "It is the judgment of the truth upon illusion, of knowledge on perception: 'It has no meaning, and does not exist.'"[14]

This kind of judgment is a sort of separating out the false from the true. I use the word "separating" quite deliberately because the Course uses it this way. Most of us think that the Course always sees the word separation as something negative, but listen to this:

> The first step toward freedom involves a sorting out of the false from the true. This is a process of *separation in the constructive sense*, and reflects the true meaning of the Apocalypse.[15] (My emphasis.)

The Course really is asking us to give up the world, but how can we give up the world while we still want it? So we must judge it first. Jesus calls for our judgment in questions like these:

> What happiness have you sought here that did not bring you pain? What moment of content has not been bought at fearful price in coins of suffering?...Be speeded on your way by honesty, and let not your experiences here deceive in retrospect. They were not free from bitter cost and joyless consequence.[16]

Judging Our Thoughts

By far the largest single category of "right judgment" is judging our thoughts. Judging our own thoughts, or being "vigilant for God and His Kingdom" as it is called in Chapter 6, covers the whole spiritual journey. Certainly it is the last phase of the spiritual journey as the Course presents it, and the first half of the journey is just preparing us and strengthening our motivation to cooperate with the Holy Spirit in this judgment process.

Let's go back to the passage about the right use of judgment quoted earlier and look at it again.[17]

The right use of judgment is not only evaluating our feelings to see how well we've done at transcending our ego, it also means to "Watch [our] mind carefully for any beliefs that hinder" the accomplishment of our goal, and step away from them.

> It has never really entered your mind to give up every idea you ever had that opposes knowledge. [But this is what we are being asked to do!] You retain thousands of little scraps of fear that prevent the Holy One from entering. Light cannot penetrate through walls you make to block it, and it is forever unwilling to destroy what you have made. No one can see through a wall, but I can step around it.[18]

The light cannot get through the wall formed by the thousands of scraps of fear in our minds. Jesus says, however, that he can step around the wall to bring us light. Does he just do that by himself, or is there some condition attached?

> Watch your mind for the scraps of fear, or you will be unable to ask me to do so.[19]

In other words, we have to judge our thoughts and notice those scraps of fear. If we leave them hidden we will be too afraid to ask for help. We have to bring them to him for healing. He goes on in the next paragraph to say,

> Be very honest with yourself in this, for we must hide nothing from each other. If you will really try to do this, you have taken the first step toward preparing your mind for the Holy One to enter.[20]

We are being called to a fearless self-appraïsal, an honest consideration of our thoughts, judging which we want to keep and which we want taken away. We are asked to "really try" to do this.

> Think honestly what you have thought that God would not have thought, and what you have not thought that God would have you think.[21]

So we are to be watching our mind for ego thoughts and judging against them. This theme comes up dozens of times in the Course.

> We said before that the Holy Spirit is evaluative, and must be. He sorts out the true from the false in your mind, and *teaches you to judge every thought you allow to enter it* in the light of what God put there.[22] (My emphasis.)

> In the mind of the thinker, then, He is judgmental, but only in order to unify the mind so it can perceive without judgment. This enables the mind to teach without judgment, and therefore to learn to *be* without judgment. The undoing is necessary only in your mind, so that you will not project, instead of extend.[23]

So He teaches us to *judge every thought* we allow to enter our minds, in order to enable us to teach without judgment and to learn to be without judgment. We are judging with Him against judgment. He is using judgment to undo judgment.

> You cannot lay aside the obstacles to real vision without looking upon them, for to lay aside means to judge against. If you will look, the Holy Spirit will judge, and He will judge truly. Yet He cannot shine away what you keep hidden, for you have not offered it to Him and He cannot take it from you.[24]

Judging Must Be With the Holy Spirit

This process of right judgment is not something we can do by ourselves; we need to cooperate with the Holy Spirit. Nor can He do it for us, without our active cooperation.

> The whole purpose of this course is to teach you that the ego is unbelievable and will forever be unbelievable. You who made the ego by believing the unbelievable cannot make this judgment alone.[25]

We need the help of the Holy Spirit to judge against the ego, but we ourselves must join with His judgment; that is the whole purpose of the Course.

> Bring, therefore, all your dark and secret thoughts to Him, and look upon them with Him. He holds the light, and you the darkness. They cannot coexist when both of You together look on them. His judgment must prevail, and He will give it to you as you join your perception to His.[26]

> If you would remember your Father, let the Holy Spirit order your thoughts and give only the answer with which He answers you.[27]

> Judge not except in quietness which is not of you.[28]

The right use of judgment, then, is to judge with the Holy Spirit, looking at the ego, its thoughts, its results in our emotions, and what it made in terms of the world, special relationships, and idols, and to judge it all as meaningless. It is to bring all such thoughts to the Holy Spirit for healing. We do not fear the ego and its thoughts; we do not make ourselves guilty for having the thoughts. We simply look at them without judging, bring them to the Holy Spirit, and allow Him to dispel them from our minds.

---

1 T-4.IV.8:5-10
2 T-7.X.6:8
3 T-4.V.1:6
4 W-pI.193.4:1-2; see also T-24.IV.5:2-3
5 T-30.I.8:2
6 T-30.I.9:2
7 T-10.III.5:1
8 T-10.III.4:7
9 T-7.VII.3:8
10 T-10.IV.2:3-4
11 T-8.I.4:1-3
12 T-8.I.5:2
13 T-2.VIII.4:3
14 T-26.III.4:3
15 T-2.VIII.4:1-2
16 T-30.V.9:7-8, 11-12
17 Read T-4.IV.8:3-10
18 T-4.III.7:1-4
19 T-4.III.7:5
20 T-4.III.8:2-3
21 T-4.IV.2:4
22 T-6.V(C).1:1-2
23 T-6.V(C).2:3-5
24 T-12.II.9:6-8; see also W- pI.136.19:1-2
25 T-7.VIII.7:1-2
26 T-14.VII.6:8-11
27 T-14.X.10:4
28 T-14.V.11:4

Chapter 9
The Last Judgment and God's Judgment

Robert

One could summarize the goal of the Course in this way: to reduce our fear of God. From its standpoint, our fear of God is what blocks us from being aware that we *are* with God. The major method for reducing our fear of God is the daily practice of forgiveness. Yet the Course also spends a great deal of effort simply trying to talk us out of this fear. It does this by reinterpreting traditional Christianity's God of judgment, and teaching instead a God of Love.

The Last Judgment

One of the most terrifying ideas to come out of Western religion is the concept of the Last Judgment. We are all familiar with this notion. At the end of the world, there will be a final trial of humanity in which God once and for all separates out the righteous from the sinners, with the result that the sinners are thrown into the lake of eternal fire and the righteous are allowed to enter into everlasting delight. The Course calls this "one of the most threatening ideas in your thinking,"[1] and for good reason: Even the most religious and upstanding among us suspect that we will not pass the test. This is an idea that increases our fear of God and so distances our minds from His Presence.

Further, the Course points out that we associate "last" with death;[2] we think that the final statement on life is death. Therefore, if it is the *last* judgment, it must be about *death*. The Course labels this "upside-down perception."[3] Its view is the reverse. What we call life—existence in time and space—is really death. Therefore, whatever stands at the end of time—the end of this living-death—must be "really the doorway to life."[4]

The Course takes great pains to redefine the Last Judgment. Aside from many scattered references, it devotes to this subject a section in the Text,[5] a "What Is" section in the Workbook[6] and a section in the Manual.[7]

The Course's new vision of the Last Judgment retains much of the framework of the traditional. Their overlap can be summarized in the form of three points: 1) At the end of time, 2) there will be a final separation between good and "evil," 3) wherein the "evil" is discarded and the good is retained and enters into eternal felicity with God.

The Course, however, has changed crucial points in the original and thus has formulated a very new concept. These differences can also be summarized in the form of three points:

1. Thoughts, not souls

Perhaps the most striking difference of all is the fact that what is separated out is not holy and sinful souls, but our own *thoughts*, our holy thoughts of love from our ego thoughts of sin. *People* are not being evaluated, only thoughts. We simply learn how to tell the difference between what is real and what is unreal.

> Here is the meeting place where thoughts are brought together; where conflicting values meet and all illusions are laid down beside the truth, where they are judged to be untrue.[8]

Thus, the Last Judgment is a final, massive application of what Allen wrote about in the last chapter: the right use of judgment.

2. We, not God, are the judge

Another comforting fact is that God does not do the judging; we do. "The Last Judgment is generally thought of as a procedure undertaken by God. Actually it will be undertaken by my brothers with my help."[9] We simply evaluate, with the help of Jesus and the Holy Spirit, which thoughts we want to keep and which we want to discard.

This, then, "reflects the true meaning of the Apocalypse."[10] When the book of Revelation speaks about God sorting out all those souls, its true meaning is that of our own minds sorting out our thoughts.

3. It is a final healing; there is no condemnation involved

This is perhaps the key point. The Last Judgment "is a final healing rather than a meting out of punishment, however much you may think that punishment is deserved."[11] It is a healing of the mind, restoring it to right-mindedness or sanity. Not only are no people condemned, but we do not even condemn our wrong thoughts. We simply judge them to be untrue. This frees us from thoughts that have been hurting us and dragging us down throughout our journey. And this release is what the Last Judgment is all about.

> You who believed that God's Last Judgment would condemn the world to hell along with you, accept this holy truth: God's Judgment is the gift of the Correction He bestowed on all your errors, freeing you from them, and all effects they ever seemed to have.[12]

An Actual Process

It is clear from the Course's many references to it and from the richness of ideas taught about it that the Last Judgment is an actual process. It is not a mere metaphor or an idea created simply to offset the traditional notion. It is really going to happen. So let us look in greater detail at what the Course describes.

The Course does make clear that the Last Judgment will occur at the very end of the spiritual journey. This of course is implied by the word "last" and by the traditional image of the Last Judgment. In this same vein, the Course teaches that the Last Judgment begins only once we have reached an exceedingly advanced state and are thus very near the end of our awakening process. In other words, it is not a process that begins now and extends to the journey's end. It does not even begin until we are almost done.

This is made clear by the fact that the Last Judgment happens *after* we have entered the real world and *after* we have experienced the Second Coming. In the section entitled "The Borderland,"[13] it says that "the final judgment" (4:2) will happen only when we reach the "borderland" (2:1), "the real world" (3:2)—a very advanced state that is basically "the journey's end" (3:1). A similar point is made in the section entitled "What Is the Second Coming?"[14] There the Second Coming is talked about in exalted terms, as "the willingness to let forgiveness rest upon all things without exception and without reserve" (1:3).

Yet even though the Second Coming "ends the lessons that the Holy Spirit teaches" (3:1), it only makes "way for the Last Judgment, in which learning ends in one last summary that will extend beyond itself, and reaches up to God" (3:1).

When we finally reach the Last Judgment what exactly will happen? Apparently, we will sift through the entire catalogue of thoughts that our minds have accumulated over the billions of years of the separation. This process is vividly described at one point:

> The Great Transformer of perception will undertake with you the careful searching of the mind that made this world, and uncover to you the seeming reasons for your making it. In the light of the real reason that He brings, as you follow Him, He will show you that there is no reason here at all.[15]

Here is the picture described: Billions of years ago we dreamt up this world for insane reasons, as part of a metaphysical psychotic break, a dissociation from true reality. Then we conveniently forgot that we had done this, and for eons upon eons wandered through the world we made, having totally forgotten we were its makers. We seemed to be living in someone else's world, strangers in a strange land, buffeted about by colossal forces as we merely tried to cook our meals, warm our hands and shelter ourselves from the elements.

Eventually, though, we turned our attention to the great journey, the long climb up the spiritual mountain, whose summit reaches beyond this world into the formless spaces of God. As we climbed we still seemed the victim of a cruel world, yet we increasingly learned that this was an illusion, and that within us lay an unshakable reality. Our entire journey, in fact, was one of learning to discern between what was real and what was illusory. Each step in our climb was another tiny advance in learning to make the choice between these two, the only choice there is.

Finally, we came very close to the summit. And now it was time for the Last Judgment. The Holy Spirit overshadowed us, and opened the vaults of our minds. He then led us on a tour through vault after vault, attic after cluttered attic, through all the billions of thoughts that lay inside our minds, most of them utterly forgotten as the decades and centuries had closed over them. Finally, He led us back to the very beginning and uncovered, there at the dawn of time, our "seeming reasons" for making the world. And now it all lay bare before us, every thought, every choice, even the astonishing memory that we were not the world's citizens; we were its makers.

Now begins the process of judging each and every thought "in the light of the real reason that He brings."[16] We judge each one in light of His proclamation "that what is false is false, and what is true has never changed,"[17] a proclamation we hear with perfect clarity for the first time. Now we see that after all the progress we have made, we still have not been sane. We still have not been able to tell the real apart from the unreal. And so we still have not fully chosen God.

But now we can, by going through the entire catalogue of our thoughts. Those thoughts that are already pure we retain. Those that are partly true we "accept and purify."[18] Those that are false entirely we reject. We calmly "disown" these thoughts, "which, without belief, will no longer exist."[19] We retain only "the blessed residue"[20]—thoughts of crystal-pure, blinding brilliance, thoughts with "no limit and no stain to mar [their] beautiful perfection."[21]

Now we are finally able to make the one judgment we have been able to make only imperfectly up until now. "It is the judgment of the truth upon illusion, of knowledge on perception: 'It has no meaning, and does not exist.'"[22] And with this, our work is done.

Having made our last judgment we no longer fear *God's* Final Judgment. And because we do not fear it, we are ready to receive it at last. Now we will hear the judgment in which there is no condemnation, no rejection, only perfect love and total inclusion. We will hear the judgment that opens wide God's Open Arms. This is a hallowed time, the end of our ancient journey. "Time pauses as eternity comes near, and silence lies across the world that everyone may hear this Judgment of the Son of God:"

> Holy are you, eternal, free and whole, at peace forever in the Heart of God. Where is the world, and where is sorrow now?[23]
>
> This is God's Final Judgment: "You are still My holy Son, forever innocent, forever loving and forever loved, as limitless as your Creator, and completely changeless and forever pure. Therefore awaken and return to Me. I am your Father and you are My Son."[24]

And as we stand upon the summit, with all clouds gone and God's Heaven opened up before us, we "will enter in and disappear into the Heart of God."[25]

God Does Not Judge, Condemn nor Punish

One of the Course's main objectives is to rid us of the idea of a judgmental, punitive God. At times it openly pleads with us to banish this idea from our minds:

> Can you believe our Father really thinks this way? It is so essential that all such thinking be dispelled that we must be sure that nothing of this kind remains in your mind.[26]

When the Course speaks of God's Judgment, strictly speaking it is not talking about judgment at all, but instead a kind of unqualified acceptance. This idea that God is punitive is not merely a relic of traditional religion. It is deeply embedded in the human psyche—which is how it got into traditional religion in the first place. The Course therefore takes care to counter all of the many ways in which we fear that God will condemn and punish us:

God will not condemn us in the end

We see the Last Judgment as God rendering His final condemnation of the condition of our soul. As we saw above, this is only our fear and is the opposite of what will really happen.

God did not kick Adam out of the garden

The Course says that the erroneous belief that sacrifice and punishment mean something to God "is responsible for a host of related errors, including the belief that God rejected Adam and forced him out of the Garden of Eden."[27] The truth is that we exiled ourselves.

God does not punish us with sickness

We think—either consciously or unconsciously—that sickness is God's punishment of us for our sins. Actually, it is our punishment of ourselves. "The ego believes that by punishing itself [with physical illness] it will mitigate the punishment of God."[28]

God does not punish us through the evils of the world

The Course mentions "...your delusion of an angry god, whose fearful image you believe you see at work in all the evils of the world."[29] The world seems to prove that God is cruel, yet He is not the one that made it. We made it to punish ourselves, since we dreamt it out of our belief in guilt—our belief that we deserve punishment.

God does not punish us through death

We see death as God's punishment of us. It is actually our punishment of ourselves in an attempt to prove that we can conquer God's eternal Life. Our "epitaph, which death itself has written...says but this: "Here lies a witness God is dead."[30]

God does not cast us into hell

We see hell as the place we deserve to spend eternity. Actually, this is the ego's goal for us, an eternity of it being free to endlessly chastise us, an eternity of us being cut off from God in a living death. "It speaks to you of Heaven, but assures you that Heaven is not for you. How can the guilty hope for Heaven?"[31]

God does not keep secrets, does not withhold from us the meaning of life

"God has no secrets. He does not lead you through a world of misery, waiting to tell you, at the journey's end, why He did this to you."[32] Actually, it is the ego that made this world, leads us through it and never tells us the real reason it did all this: it was trying to defeat us.

God does not wait to give us our reward

We think that God is constantly stalling to give us our just reward, perhaps even waiting until after we die. Yet this waiting is produced by our own ambivalence, which fears—and so holds off—the blessing that God has already given. "Given a change of purpose for the good, there is no reason for an interval in which disaster strikes, to be perceived as 'good' some day but now in form of pain."[33]

God did not crucify Jesus as punishment for our sins

"I was not 'punished' because *you* were bad."[34]

The Holy Spirit's teaching and guidance do not ask sacrifice of us

We think the Holy Spirit asks us to sacrifice everything that is fun and pleasurable. Actually, He only asks us to give up what hurts us (which, alas, includes things we consider fun and pleasurable). "You no more recognize what is painful than you know what is joyful, and are, in fact, very apt to confuse the two...The Holy Spirit never asks for sacrifice, but the ego always does."[35]

---

1 T-2.VIII.2:1
2 T-2.VIII.5:1
3 T-2.VIII.5:2
4 T-2.VIII.5:3
5 T-2.VIII
6 W-pII.10
7 M-15
8 T-26.III.2:3
9 T-2.VIII.3:1-2
10 T-2.VIII.4:2
11 T-2.VIII.3:3
12 W-pII.10.3:1
13 T-26.III
14 W-pII.9
15 T-17.II.5:2-3
16 T-17.II.5:3
17 W-pII.10.1:1
18 T-6.V(C)1:4
19 T-2.VIII.4:5
20 T-5.V.2:2
21 M-23.5:7
22 T-26.III.4:3
23 M-15.1:10-12
24 W-pII.10.5:1-3
25 W-pII.14.5:5
26 T-3.I.2:8-9
27 T-3.I.3:9
28 T-5.V.5:6
29 W-pI.153.7:3
30 W-pI.163.5:2-3
31 T-15.I.3:6-7
32 T-22.I.3:10-11
33 T-26.VIII.7:9
34 T-3.I.2:10
35 T-7.X.3:4; 5:5

Chapter 10

Letting Go of Judgment

Allen

Some Tools or Learning Devices

The Course mentions three primary means for teaching us its lessons: the holy instant, the holy relationship, and the Holy Spirit's guidance.[1] Each of them plays a part in letting judgment go.

The Holy Instant

When our learning begins, our minds are operating from the ego's frame of reference. Therefore, we need practice sessions in which we can temporarily adopt an alternate frame of mind. Once we experience this new state of mind we will want to spend more and more of our time in it, until eventually it becomes *all* that we want.

The holy instant enables us to temporarily reach this new state of mind. One purpose of the holy instant is to suspend judgment entirely.[2] (I suggest you read the whole paragraph this quote is taken from.)

> The holy instant reflects His knowing by bringing all perception out of the past, thus removing the frame of reference you have built by which to judge your brothers.[3]

When we practice a holy instant, we choose to set aside the past and, just for a moment, to suspend judgment. Our past judgments do not concern us, nor do we worry about the fact that we will judge again in five minutes; for this instant, we attempt to let it go. All we are doing is "trying on" the new frame of reference. This is not a final commitment; we can take our judgment back the second that practice is over. If we want to.

The Course recognizes that we are afraid of letting judgment go and of giving up the past as a reference point. We are terrified of losing the frame of reference that the ego has provided because we think that "without the ego, all would be chaos."[4] We fear having no frame of reference at all. Jesus, however, assures us that "without the ego, all would be love."[5] There will be another frame of reference to take the ego's place. The holy instant provides a safe way for us to experience this without making a total commitment.

The word "suspend" is interesting because it implies something temporary. When we suspend judgment we don't give it up forever (although that is the eventual goal, of course). We just withhold it temporarily, and see what happens. What happens is that the judgment of the Holy Spirit rushes in to take its place. Jesus knows that if we allow ourselves to see with the Holy Spirit's perception, even for an instant, we won't be able to go back; not completely. It's like the "figure-ground" illustrations. Once we see the second picture it is hard to imagine *not* seeing it again.

The early Workbook lessons emphasize the need to suspend judgment about the objects you select to practice with. For instance, read the first two paragraphs of Lesson 3.

So we can start with simple things. Just keep reminding yourself during the day: "I don't know what this means. I do not know what the purpose of this is. I do not know what anything is for." To say, "I do not know," is to suspend judgment.

Later Workbook exercises instruct you to pick a person, allow yourself to recognize your judgments about them, and then to practice letting those judgments go. Jesus knows you need practice to learn to let go of judgment. The Workbook is a practice manual for having holy instants in which judgment is suspended.

Think again of the figure-ground drawing. The first time you try it can take a long time to see the second image. But once you've done it, the second drawing becomes easier, and the third even easier. Why? Because you've learned the technique of letting go of what your eyes tell you at first and letting another perception take its place. That is what the practice of holy instants does: it trains you in the technique of suspending judgment.

The Holy Relationship

Relationships are a great teaching device. Can you think of any better place to practice letting judgment go than in your relationships?

In the holy instant the focus is on suspending judgment and letting go of the past as a frame of reference. In the holy relationship, another factor gets added in. We get to practice seeing things from the perspective of unity instead of separateness. We get to practice the fact that what we think directly affects the other person. In a holy relationship we are learning in microcosm what is true in the macrocosm: that all minds are joined. We start practicing with one other individual. If we learn to let go of judgment with one person, we will have learned how to do so with the whole world.

The Text speaks of practicing the holy instant *in* the holy relationship.[6] We offer the Holy Spirit our willingness to let Him "exchange" our unholy instant of judgment, when peace is threatened, for a holy instant. We open ourselves up for that change in the frame of reference for both participants. We seek the holy instant to *share it*. We are learning that it is not possible to have it without the other, but that "It will come to both at the request of either."[7]

The Holy Spirit's Guidance

We've seen that relinquishing judgment is the prerequisite to hearing the Voice for God. We have to let go of our definition of what things are for in order to hear His answer to our questions. If we are looking for guidance we are *forced* to learn to give up judgment. The whole area of learning to be guided is thus a great classroom for giving up judgment.

> Have you yet learned to stand aside and hear the Voice of Judgment in yourself? Or do you still attempt to take His role from Him? Learn to be quiet, for His Voice is heard in stillness. And His Judgment comes to all who stand aside in quiet listening, and wait for Him.[8]

We think the whole purpose of guidance is telling us where to go and what to do. A deeper, underlying purpose is to teach us to let go of our judgments. Guidance is not just about where to live, or finding the best job or the best love partner. Those are also the tools the Holy

Spirit uses in His larger purpose of teaching us to let go of our judgment about everything, and to return the function of judgment to Him.

We judge because we are projecting guilt. Following the guidance of the Holy Spirit, or allowing Him to judge for us, is the way to be absolved of guilt, and thus free ourselves from the need to judge. Why does following His guidance free us from guilt? Because our guilt comes from usurping the functions of God. Just as it is God's function to decide who we are in Heaven, so it is the Holy Spirit's function to decide what we do with our lives on earth. In usurping His function of judgment we have made ourselves guilty. To return the function of judgment back to the Holy Spirit, Whose function it is, is the way out of that guilt.[9]

We don't want to go overboard in seeking guidance. The Course disputes the false idea that we should ask guidance in every second. The Course says that such detailed seeking of guidance simply isn't practical:

> To ask the Holy Spirit to decide for you is simply to accept your true inheritance. Does this mean that you cannot say anything without consulting Him? No, indeed! That would hardly be practical, and it is the practical with which this course is most concerned.[10]

The same advice is hinted at back in Chapter 30, "Rules for Decision," where it says: "It is not wise to let yourself become preoccupied with every step you take."[11] Probably, however, most of us are in no danger yet of going overboard. We need to learn to make it a habit to ask for guidance a lot more than we are now.

What *are* we supposed to do then?

> If you have made it a habit to ask for help when and where you can, you can be confident that wisdom will be given you when you need it. Prepare for this each morning, remember God when you can throughout the day, ask the Holy Spirit's help when it is feasible to do so, and thank Him for His guidance at night. And your confidence will be well founded indeed.[12]

That's pretty clear. Prepare your mind in the morning, along the lines of the Workbook lesson, listening to receive His plan. Whenever you can through the day, remember God and ask for help from the

Holy Spirit. And when the day is done, at night pause again to thank Him for His guidance. Keep doing this until it becomes a habit, and you will have all the guidance you need, when you need it.

Review of Some Helpful Thoughts

Realizing You Don't Know

One foundational practice is reminding ourselves that we don't know what anything is for, nor how to respond to it. For example, when some problem arises and we think we need to make a judgment, the Workbook advises us:

> Be not deceived by the form of problems today. Whenever any difficulty seems to rise, tell yourself quickly:
>
> *Let me recognize this problem so it can be solved.*
>
> Then try to suspend all judgment about what the problem is. If possible, close your eyes for a moment and ask what it is. You will be heard and you will be answered.[13]

In other words, as was said in Chapter 7, you don't even know what the problem is, much less know the answer. Instead of asking for an answer to the problem as you see it, ask what the problem is!

Recognizing the Cost of Judgment

Jesus says that he is trying to teach us to associate pain with the ego and joy with the Holy Spirit. He wants us to recognize what following our own judgments is costing us so that we will be *willing* to let them go. A good example can be seen in the Manual, in "How is Judgment Relinquished?"[14]

Sharing Perception with the Holy Spirit

We ask the Holy Spirit to share His perception with us. We suspend our judgment and ask His to take its place. When we find ourselves judging, just bring those thoughts to the Holy Spirit. When we bring darkness to light, darkness is dispelled. "Bring, therefore, all your dark and secret thoughts to Him, and look upon them with Him."[15]

Perhaps one of the most difficult times in which to give up judgment is when you feel deeply hurt by someone you loved. When you believe you have been wrongfully and unfairly treated, the hurt and pain you feel makes forgiving seem almost impossible. At times like these, one of my favorite passages from the Text is found in "The Fear of Redemption," seventh paragraph.[16]

In simple words, tell Him about it. Share your perception, and ask for His. It always works for me. No matter what you share He will not be shocked. Just exposing my muddled mind to Him brings healing.

Workbook Lesson 347 starts by reminding us that judgment is a weapon that we use against ourselves to keep the miracle away. Remember the sword of judgment, keeping love out of the space we have put between ourselves and our brothers? In using the sword of judgment we are fighting against our own will, *mistakenly believing we want separation*. Our mind is confused at the roots.

I love these two sentences because of their stark simplicity:

> Straighten my mind, my Father. It is sick.[17]

There is a science fiction novel by Zenna Henderson, called *The People*. It is about some beings who looked just like humans but had actually escaped from a planet that was being destroyed. They came here to live on earth. They lived very simply, almost like the Amish, but they had telepathic abilities. Certain people among them, called "sorters," had intense empathic senses and were able to enter into other people's minds when they were distraught and "sort" their thoughts out for them.

I remember weeping as I read those stories. I wanted so much to have somebody who could sort my mind for me! I felt so confused sometimes. Finally, one day, I found myself praying to God and saying, "Father, sort me! Sort my thoughts, and bring order and peace in my mind."

That is exactly the idea here. "Straighten my mind, my Father. It is sick." We need to pray like that when we get caught up in judgment. We need to get right down to brass tacks and say, "My mind is sick. Help!"

How do we get our minds sorted? We "give all judgment to the One [God] gave to judge for [us],"[18] the Holy Spirit. We share our perception with Him.

> He sees what I behold, and yet He knows the truth. He looks on pain, and yet He understands it is not real, and in His understanding is it healed. He gives the miracles my dreams would hide from my awareness. Let Him judge today.[19]

He looks at the mess, the horror, the problem, the sickness, the difficulty, the grievous loss, the animosity, or whatever it is; He sees what I see *and yet He knows the truth.* He sees what I see, and yet somehow He is still serene and joyful. He understands the illusion is not real. I don't know how to understand that, but He does, and He can see for me. I can share the tranquillity of His perception if I am willing to let Him judge for me.

Just Move in That Direction

We spent a lot of time looking at how pervasive judgment is. Maybe you're feeling by now, "My God! How will I ever be free from judgment? How can I ever let it go?" The only thing really necessary is that we *desire* that judgment be undone.

> Vision would not be necessary had judgment not been made. Desire now its whole undoing, and it is done for you.[20]

All we need to do is to be willing to move in that direction:

> What, then, is the function of the teacher of God in this concluding lesson? He need merely learn how to approach it; to be willing to go in its direction. He need merely trust that, if God's Voice tells him it is a lesson he can learn, he can learn it. He does not judge it either as hard or easy. His Teacher points to it, and he trusts that He will show him how to learn it.[21]

> Undoing is not your task. But it is up to you to welcome it or not.[22]

Just "be willing to go in its direction." Don't worry about how you will get there; the means will be provided by the Holy Spirit. The undoing of judgment is His task. Just move in that direction, to the best of your ability. Your little ability will be augmented by His infinite ability, and you will move much faster than you think—if you are willing.

We look at letting go of judgment and what do you think we do? Can you guess? *We judge it*! We judge it to be difficult. Or maybe we judge it to be easy, and underestimate the tenacity of our egos. So, let us start our practice here: Don't judge how hard or easy it is to let go of judgment. Just start moving in that direction, trusting the Holy Spirit that He will show us how to do it.

> And now sit down in true humility, and realize that all God would have you do you can do. Do not be arrogant and say you cannot learn His Own curriculum. His Word says otherwise. His Will be done. It cannot be otherwise. And be you thankful it is so.[23]

---

1 T-18.V.1:3
2 T-15.V.1:2
3 T-15.V.9:3
4 T-15.V.1:6
5 T-15.V.1:7
6 T-18.V.6:1-6; 7:1-6
7 T-18.V.6:7
8 M-15.2:10-13
9 M-29:3:3-10
10 M-29.5:8-10
11 T-30.I.1:4
12 M-29.5:4-10
13 W-pI.79.10:1-6
14 M-10.6:1-11
15 T-14.VII.6:8
16 T-13.III.7
17 W-pII.347.1:2-3
18 W-pII.347.1:5
19 W-pII.347.1:6-9
20 T-20.VIII.1:5-6
21 M-14.4:4-8
22 T-21.II.8:5
23 M-14.5:10-15

The Circle's Mission Statement

To discern the author's vision of *A Course in Miracles* and manifest that in our lives, in the lives of students, and in the world.

1

To faithfully discern the author's vision of *A Course in Miracles.*

In interpreting the Course we strive for total fidelity to its words and the meanings they express. We thereby seek to discover the Course as the author saw it.

2

To be an instrument in Jesus' plan to manifest his vision of the Course in the lives of students and in the world.

We consider this to be Jesus' organization and therefore we attempt to follow his guidance in all we do. Our goal is to help students understand, as well as discern for themselves, the Course's thought system as he intended, and use it as he meant it to be used – as a literal program in spiritual awakening. Through doing so we hope to help ground in the world the intended way of doing the Course, here at the beginning of its history.

3

To help spark an enduring tradition based entirely on students joining together in doing the Course as the author envisioned.

We have a vision of local Course support systems composed of teachers, students, healers, and groups, all there to support one another in making full use of the Course. These support systems, as they continue and multiply, will together comprise an enduring spiritual tradition, dedicated solely to doing the Course as the author intended. Our goal is to help spark this tradition, and to assist others in doing the same.

4

To become an embodiment, a birthplace of this enduring spiritual tradition.

To help spark this tradition we must first become a model for it ourselves. This requires that we at the Circle follow the Course as our individual path; that we ourselves learn forgiveness through its program. It requires that we join with each other in a group holy relationship dedicated to the common goal of awakening through the Course. It also requires that we cultivate a local support system here in Sedona, and that we have a facility where others could join with us in learning this approach to the Course. Through all of this we hope to become a seed for an ongoing spiritual tradition based on *A Course in Miracles*.

Books & Booklets in this Series

Commentaries on *A Course in Miracles*
By Robert Perry and Allen Watson

1. **Seeing the Face of Christ in All Our Brothers** *by Perry*. How we can see the Presence of God in others. $5.00

3. **Shrouded Vaults of the Mind** *by Perry*. Draws a map of the mind based on the Course, and takes you on a tour through its many levels. $5.00

4. **Guidance: Living the Inspired Life** *by Perry*. Sketches an overall perspective on guidance and its place on the spiritual path. $7.00

6. **Reality & Illusion: An Overview of Course Metaphysics, Part I** *by Perry*. Examines the Course's vision of reality. With booklet #7, forms a comprehensive overview of the Course's metaphysical thought system. $5.00

7. **Reality & Illusion: An Overview of Course Metaphysics, Part II** *by Perry*. Discusses the origins of our apparent separation from God. $5.00

8. **A Healed Mind Does Not Plan** *by Watson*. Examines our approach to planning and decision-making, showing how it is possible to leave the direction of our lives up to the Holy Spirit. $5.00

9. **Through Fear to Love** *by Watson*. Explores two sections from the Course that deal with our fear of redemption. Leads the reader to see how it is possible to look upon ourselves with love. $5.00

10. **The Journey Home** *by Watson*. Presents a description of our spiritual destination and what we must go through to get there. $5.00

11. **Everything You Always Wanted to Know About Judgment but Were Too Busy Doing It to Notice** *by Perry and Watson*. A survey of various teachings about judgment in the Course. $8.00

12. **The Certainty of Salvation** *by Perry and Watson*. How we can become certain that we will find our way to God. $5.00

13. **What is Death?** *by Watson*. The Course's view of what death really is. $5.00

14. **The Workbook as a Spiritual Practice** *by Perry*. A guide for getting the most out of the Workbook. $5.00

15. **I Need Do Nothing: Finding the Quiet Center** *by Watson*. An in-depth discussion of one of the most misunderstood sections of the Course. $5.00

16. **A Course Glossary** *by Perry*. 150 definitions of terms and phrases from the Course for students and study groups. $7.00

17. **Seeing the Bible Differently: How *A Course in Miracles* Views the Bible** *by Watson*. Shows the similarities, differences, and continuity between the Course and the Bible. $6.00

18. **Relationships as a Spiritual Journey: From Specialness to Holiness** *by Perry*. Describes the Course's unique view of how we can find God through the transformation of our relationships. $10.00

19. **A Workbook Companion Volume I** *by Watson and Perry*. Commentaries on Lessons 1 -120. $16.00

20. **A Workbook Companion Volume II** *by Watson and Perry*. Commentaries on Lessons 121 - 243. $16.00

21. **A Workbook Companion Volume III** *by Watson and Perry*. Commentaries on Lessons 244 - 365. $18.00

22. **The Answer Is a Miracle** *by Perry and Watson*. Looks at what the Course means by miracles, and how we can experience them in our lives. $7.00

23. **Let Me Remember You** *by Perry and Watson*. Regaining a sense of God's relevance, both in the Course and in our lives. $10.00

24. **Bringing the Course to Life: How to Unlock the Meaning of *A Course in Miracles* for Yourself** *by Watson and Perry*. Designed to teach the student, through instruction, example and exercises, how to read the Course so that the experience becomes a personal encounter with the truth. $12.00

For shipping rates, a complete catalog of our products and services, or for information about events, please contact us at:

The Circle of Atonement
Teaching and Healing Center
P.O. Box 4238
W. Sedona, AZ 86340
(928) 282-0790, Fax (928) 282-0523
e-mail: info@circleofa.com
website: http://nen.sedona.net/circleofa/